P. M. Johnson

Life Among the Hindus

P. M. Johnson

Life Among the Hindus

ISBN/EAN: 9783743364585

Manufactured in Europe, USA, Canada, Australia, Japa

Cover: Foto ©Suzi / pixelio.de

Manufactured and distributed by brebook publishing software (www.brebook.com)

P. M. Johnson

Life Among the Hindus

Life Among the Hindus.

BEING A JOURNAL OF DAILY EXPERIENCES AND OBSERVATIONS DURING TWO YEARS OF LIFE, LABOR AND TRAVEL AMONG THE PEOPLES OF INDIA.

— BY —

REV. P. M. JOHNSON, M. A.,

MISSIONARY TO THE TELUGUS.

ST. LOUIS:
C. B. Woodward Company.
1893.

To my wife, who, far more than myself, has had to suffer for Christ, this little volume is most affectionately dedicated.

CONTENTS.

	PAGE.
CHAPTER I.	
The Departure and Voyage	9
CHAPTER II.	
Introduction to Life in India	15
CHAPTER III.	
Language and Customs	25
CHAPTER IV.	
A Hindu Wedding: Hot Winds	41
CHAPTER V.	
Across the Burning Sands: Famine	49
CHAPTER VI.	
Origin of Idolatry: Religion of the Hindus	59
CHAPTER VII.	
Degeneration, the Fruit of Idolatry	75

CONTENTS.

	PAGE.
CHAPTER VIII.	
Persecution: Mohammedanism	87
CHAPTER IX.	
The Telugu Mission: Its Beginning and Struggles	105
CHAPTER X.	
The Break of Day: Triumph of the Gospel	111
CHAPTER XI.	
Shadows begin to Deepen: Sickness and Death	125
CHAPTER XII.	
The Sad Farewell: Homeward Voyage: Storm at Sea	143

INTRODUCTION.

The substance of the following pages has been delivered in the form of lectures a number of times since our return from India. It has been thought, if put in book form, it might reach hundreds of people more than would ever have opportunity of hearing the lectures, and so impart that information which would lead to a far deeper interest in the great cause of the world's evangelization. In the composition, with reference to both the style and the arrangement, an effort has been made to make it a volume of practical information, especially for those who may not have the opportunity of reading more extensively concerning the things mentioned in these sketches.

We hope these pages may be used of God to bring our people nearer in prayer and in sympathy to the millions of their Hindu brothers and sisters; and we earnestly pray that, if it be God's will, some who read here may be led to go in his name, "To give light to them who sit in darkness and in the shadow of death, to guide their feet into the way of peace."

P. M. JOHNSON.

August 11, 1893.

CHAPTER I.

THE DEPARTURE AND VOYAGE.

The last farewell had been said, and we walked somewhat restlessly up and down the deck of the "Scythia," waiting for the signal of departure from the homeland. Just at 1 o'clock, P. M., October 4, 1890, we moved slowly out of the Boston harbor into the Atlantic. We watched the last dim outlines of our native country go down in the western horizon, and then turned to look through our silent tears upon the broad ocean before us.

The mingled hopes and fears, joys and sorrows which then filled our hearts, no one can ever tell; and none, save those who have experienced them, may ever know. But the Lord who said to us "Go," was indeed with us, was our strength and comfort. The voyage to Liverpool was, altogether, very pleasant; there being a number of other missionaries with us. That unmerciful monster, sea-sickness, would insist on keeping us company, and very often we had to leave a richly laden table to pay our respects to him.

As we had to wait two weeks in England, the time was very pleasantly and profitably spent in sightseeing in the great metropolis, and other historical parts of the wonderful old island of Britain. Among other things, we shall never forget the hour spent in Spurgeon's Tabernacle, listening to the "wonderful words of life" from the lips of the greatest preacher since the days of the Apostles. He, in fact, preached with the power and demonstration of the Spirit. We sat in the midst of an audience of six thousand, when Spurgeon came forward, he said in a loud voice: "Let us worship God," and began his prayer: "Our Lord, make us abundant in that child-like spirit which submits to the will of the Father." The whole character of the man was certainly revealed in those words.

> For this the secret fountain of his wealth,
> He sought to know and do his Father's will.

This good man whose heart ever yearned for the lost of his people, sleeps now in

The grave of England's greatest, noblest child,
And he that trusted, leaning on his God,
Shall speak, though dead, and dead, shall yet outlive
Ten thousand of his fellows living yet.

October 25th, we boarded the "Clan McArthur," headed for India. Our course was southward through the Bay of Biscay and thence through the Straits of Gibraltar. A magnificent scene in passing this strait. We entered near midnight,

And there we saw in moonlight pale
Old Afric's northern mountain crests
Like hugest ghosts in somber vail,
Rise up from that dark continent.
Gibraltar's famous rocks arose,
Like monuments divinely built;
Sought in the moonlight to disclose
The solemn grandeur of the hour.
Here dimly burnt the beacon lights,
Out in the hazy distance shone;
And weird and solemn all the sights
That moved the hearts upon our ship.

Onward over the Mediterranean Sea sighting Algiers, we came upon the island of Malta, or Mileta, where Paul was shipwrecked. A half-day was spent in looking over this interesting island. Our next landing was Port Said, the entrance to the Suez Canal.

Here we get our first sight of real heathenism. Men and boys crowd around us, some with a kind of loose sack thrown over their bodies, suspended by a draw-string around the neck. The people here, as in most of northern Africa, are chiefly Mohammedan in religion.

The passage through the Suez Canal, about a hundred miles, is very interesting. Passing on through the sandy desert, constantly traversed by camels between Assyria and Egypt, we came to the Bitter Lakes. They are supposed to be part of the northern arm of the Red Sea, when it extended much farther north than it now does. The passage through the Red Sea would be delightful were it not so exceedingly hot, as it usually is. Off to our left, in Arabia, was the Sinai range of mountains, while on the right, the African hill tops, near sunset, are lit up by the rosy tints from the gorgeous array of clouds that surround the sun in his going down, and reflect a beautiful sheen over the waters where once, upon dry land, the chosen of God passed safely over.

Through the Red Sea, the Gulf of Aden, the Indian ocean, we landed next on Ceylon, the island of spices and of Buddhist idolatry. Truly this is one of the most beautiful islands of the sea. Luxuriant vegetation, the best of tropical fruits, and beautiful flowers, abound every where and all the time. And all this beauty of nature is only marred by the numberless Buddhist temples, over which the soft, scent-laden breezes mingle with their rustling music the din of heathen worship.

Truly the poet hath written:

> What though the spicy breezes
> Blow soft o'er Ceylon's isle,
> Where every prospect pleases,
> And only man is vile?
> In vain with lavish kindness
> The gifts of God are strown;
> The heathen in his blindness,
> Bows down to wood and stone.

Three days more brought us to India; and here we are, after two months of travel, sight-seeing and waiting, worn and weary, at our journey's end.

CHAPTER II.

The Introduction to Life in India.

We came into the Madras harbor at night, and had to wait for morning dawn to go ashore. The sun rose clear and bright over the Bay of Bengal. With great eagerness we rose to get the first sight of the country which was, henceforth, to be our home. The harbor was already filled with small boats, and men and boys crying out the sale of their goods, or inviting us to go ashore in their boats. They were as dark as the Indians of the West; having, most of them, long, coarse black hair, clearly outlined features, medium height, or smaller, and with little or no clothing on their slender bodies. The city of Madras lay out before us, not very inviting. There are a few nice government and other buildings, but the native city is a continuous number of mud huts set closely together. The streets are narrow and very filthy.

We were met on the steamer by Revs. Drake, Downie and Heinrichs, who greeted us with a hearty welcome. They brought us letters of welcome from most of our missionaries in India, and assisted us in getting ourselves and baggage ashore, and our baggage through the Custom House. By this time we were feeling the heat of the sun and were glad to arrive, at last, in the pleasant Perambur bungalow, where a good breakfast was awaiting us. It will be remembered that in India it is customary among missionaries to have four meals a day. A very light meal, called *chotta hazaree*, at six or seven in the morning; breakfast at ten or eleven; a cup of tea with English biscuits or fruit at three o'clock, and dinner at six in the evening. This suits the hot climate better than our American style. Mr. and Mrs. Drake, by their kindness, made us feel quite at home, and we enjoyed two days' rest in their house. During this time we looked over the city a little, and acquainted ourselves with some of the polite tradesmen. Enter a shop to buy a topie, or sun hat, and ask the price of it. The answer will be: "Twelve rupees, master, twelve rupees; this is a first class topie, sir." "O, I can't pay so much for this topie." "How much, master give, sir; how much give?" "Tell me proper prices." "Give me nine rupees?" "No, I can't give so much." "Well, tell how much give; master knows price." "I'll give you four rupees." "Can't take four rupees; good topie, sir; see." "Well, I'll go somewhere else and buy." "All right sir, take sir, never mind." And thus you have your hat after wasting enough time and talk to have bought forty acres of land. But such is Hindu custom.

Though in Madras, we were yet a long way from Ongole, the station to which we had been appointed. After a little rest, much needed and greatly enjoyed, we then took the train for Nellore. The whole day was occupied by the journey of about one hundred and fifty miles. A little after dark we walked into the Nellore compound where we were greeted with a song of welcome from the school children, and were made at home with our dear friends, Mr. and Mrs. Heinrichs, who were then temporarily stationed in Nellore with Dr. Downie. We spent Sunday with them, and enjoyed our first privilege of speaking, through an interpreter, to the Telugus. The mission houses, with flowers always in bloom, yards shaded by evergreens, casurina, margosa trees and tall mangoes, were, indeed, resting places in a weary land. From Nellore to our next stopping place we are fully initiated into the native style of travel in India. We had about forty miles to go this stage and, as the days are too hot for travel, we must make the journey at night. About four o'clock our man, Chinniya, whom we had engaged to be our cook, brought up the cart in which Mrs. Johnson and myself were to make the trip to Ramapatam. A cart of two wheels, a kind of frame covered over with bamboo matting, inside of which we were to make our bed of straw. The thing was crowded nearly full of our baggage, and then we were to wedge ourselves in the best way possible. All was ready at length, and the "bandy man" tied up his two little oxen to the cart and we were off, jolting and jigging along. We fared splendidly until late at night when we were tired, and it began raining. Our covering was not sufficient to turn all the rain, and our bed was not more pleasant than a Pullman sleeper. The rain was slightly chilling to the driver, and he was inclined to crawl back as far into the cart as possible. Then, occasionally, he would get sleepy and, while nodding, the oxen would stop.

We knew only one word in Telugu, and had learned that for the special occasion. So I would rise up and call out to the driver, "poni," which means, let them go. He would jump like he was shot at, utter a sleepy groan, and then mutter something to the oxen; so on we would go for a little while. But the force of my "poni" would not last long. About the time we began to doze a little the cart would stop; and hour after hour in the rain and mud, I had to get up and urge the procession on, until my little word "*poni*" was nearly worn out. When the novelty of the occassion didn't amuse us, I really wished for a few more Telugu words to express certain thoughts of tenderness toward that sleepy man and his oxen. You know I could but sympathize with them. Morning dawned and we were yet ten miles from even a rest house where we could stop, sheltered from the burning rays of the sun. But the rain had ceased, and we had better control of the oxen. So about half-past ten we came into Cavili, a village yet twelve miles from Ramapatam. Mrs. Johnson was almost exhausted, and I fancy I resembled a Comanchee just off a long hunt. We had begun to despair of our future, when, as we drove up into this village, we heard a voice in clear English, "Is Mr. and Mrs. Johnson here?" It sounded like the voice of an angel. We looked out from our close quarters and there was Miss Cummings, the lady missionary from Ramapatam. She had anticipated our troubles and had come to meet us. She had brought for us Dr. Boggs' English phaeton, drawn by eight strong men. O! what a relief from the old cart. But when rested we were glad of the experience. After two or three hours in the rest house and a good lunch, we started, as it was cloudy, on our way to Ramapatam where we arrived about five o'clock in the evening, thanking God that we were alive.

After a day's rest in Ramapatam, we must make one more stage ere we reached the end of our journey and rest in our own house. But this stage was quite pleasantly made, as we had the phaeton the rest of the way. Chinniya could speak a little English and, through him, we changed coolies, or men; as in such travel we have to pay the old company and get new men every ten miles. We pay them four annas each, or ten cents a stage. As it was cloudy we made this run to Ongole in the day time and arrived there a little after dark. Dr. Clough gave us a most hearty welcome, and we remained in his house until our own was arranged and ready for occupancy. Dr. Clough's mission house is a real pleasant one. A large yard, well shaded with margosa trees, a number of other buildings, including the chapel, two small bungalows and the girls' boarding school. Here, also, is the beautiful baptistry, or pool, where so many have been baptized. The high school bungalow, about a quarter of a mile to the southeast, was to be our home. It was considerably dilapidated, and we had to wait till it was partially repaired. By and by, everything was arranged and we moved in. Now comes the interesting experience of hiring servants. We know nothing about it, don't know how many we need; but the missionaries all tell us we must have servants. We can't do our own work in that hot country. But we already have a cook, and as he can speak a little English and seems rather shrewd, we put him in the lead and ask him what we must do. A dozen or more men and women have already gathered around the house, applying for positions. Chinniya assumes an air of importance, as only a Hindoo in authority can do, and demands of each one of the applicants what he can do, and how much their former masters paid them. They all rise as quickly as if a cobra was after them, and make their salaams and bow nearly to the ground two or three times. Then each comes forward with his papers, if he has any, and I read them. They are most likely from missionaries whom they have served. Many of them have but little idea what is written on their papers; some of them are pretty good, and others not so flattering, and some actually mentioning the misconduct for which they were discharged. But they fancy because it is a paper it must be all right. Out of the number we select first a "matey," a young man to assist the cook, and wait on the table. Next an "ayah," a woman to wait on Mrs. Johnson, and assist in keeping the house straight; then a water carrier, and lastly, a sweeper. We announce to the company our selections, and the chosen make a nice bow while the others begin to fall down on their faces and cry "*aygah, tundree, tundree! naku puni ladu!*" (Sir, father, father, I have no work.) But give them a small present, five cents, to buy their rice for that day and they go away quite happy. Now, we must agree on the salaries of those selected. But we look at the five standing before us; we remonstrate against having so many servants. Two men could easily do all our work. But no, sir; they each have their separate work, and all the gold of Ophir could'nt hire a cook or a matey to sweep. It is not their custom, and that settles it. We must have a separate man or woman for each department of the work. And everybody says we must have them, can't live in India and have our health without them. So how much does the matey want per month? Well, the story of the sun hat must be repeated. He thinks he can do better work than anyone else and declares he never will steal, like all others do; he is the only perfectly honest man in his country. He wants nine rupees. But we have anticipated these difficulties and informed ourselves about salaries. So, to make matters short, we say, "Five rupees is enough for you; if you can't work for that we will call some one else." "Very well, sir." The same experience is gone through with all the others. The experienced ayah gets six rupees a month, the water carrier two, and the sweeper two. They all always board themselves. (The government rupee is worth about forty cents.) Now, our housekeeping machinery is set in motion.

CHAPTER III.

THE LANGUAGE AND CUSTOMS.

The experience of a missionary on his arrival in India, is rather amusing. The native Christians must crowd around him almost everytime he steps out of the house. They all make their polite salaams and have a thousand questions to ask. So they begin with their bombardment of questions, never thinking in their excitement and joy that it is all Dutch to the missionary. There he stands, after he has said his salaam, and can go no further. By and by, some one happens to think that the missionary doesn't know Telugu, and in a voice above all the others, announces his discovery. Then both the missionary and the Telugus enjoy a hearty laugh at each other's awkwardness in the situation.

After the housekeeping is arranged, the next thing is the employment of a "*munshi*," or native teacher. You will already have had a number of applicants with their papers, if they have ever been employed in the work before. You make your selection, agree on a salary, usually ten or fifteen rupees a month, and begin work at once. Your teacher, next morning, enters the room, in new cloth, and pompously addresses you, "Good morning, your honor; I hope your honor will be quite well this morning." He then comes down from "your honor" to assume that you know absolutely nothing—and maybe you don't know very much—and begins with you like you were a four year old child. After he has talked on for fifteen or twenty minutes, using all the swelling words in English he can command, you are getting a little tired and tell him you understand all that, to come down to business and give you an introduction to the Telugu alphabet. Then you must teach him how to teach you, or he will talk for a whole day all around the subject, going off into Sanscrit and trying more to display his own learning than to impart instruction to you. The alphabet is the most difficult part of the Telugu, excepting, perhaps, the pronunciation of words of Sanscrit origin. There are in common use in the alphabet forty-eight primary characters, thirty-five consonants and thirteen vowels. These characters are so combined as to make over four hundred and fifty letters. Besides these, there are enough signs and letters in all to make over five hundred characters in the Telugu alphabet. But the alphabet once mastered, as each letter has only one sound and each word is spelled just as pronounced, the spelling and reading is quite easy. The Telugu is a beautiful poetic language; called the "Italian of the East." It is of Dravidian origin and is much mixed with Sanscrit. The following hymn, "Nothing but the Blood of Jesus," in Telugu and Roman characters, is given as a sample of the Telugu, the language spoken by about seventeen millions of people on the eastern coast along the Bay of Bengal, between Madras and Vizagapatam and extending westward toward Goa—about half the peninsula.

"Nothing But the Blood of Jesus."

యేసు రక్తము మాత్రము.

ఏది పాపం తిసును ?   యేసు రక్తం మాత్రం ;
పది స్వస్థపర్చును ?   యేసు రక్తం మాత్రం.

హాది వ్యరక్తము   ఆ బుగ్గ వినహా !
వేరేమి లేదుగా   యేసు రక్తం మాత్రం.

ఇకబలి చాలును,   యేసు రక్తం మాత్రం,
నాకు సమాధానము,   యేసు రక్తం మాత్రం.

పాపికి ఆశ్రయము,   యేసు రక్తం మాత్రం ;
పాపపు వారము,   యేసు రక్తం మాత్రం.

పది శుద్ధి చేసును,   యేసు రక్తం మాత్రం ;
పది శాంతపర్చును.   యేసు రక్తం మాత్రం.

1. Adi papum thesunu,
   Yasu racthum mathrum;
   Adi swastha partsunu,
   Yasu racthum mathrum.

   Chorus: Ha devyah racthamu!
   A bugga vinnaha!
   Vwarami laduga,
   Yasu racthum mathrum.

2. Ikabali tsalunu,
   Yasu racthum mathrum;
   Naku samadhanamu,
   Yasu racthum mathrum.

3. Papiki ashrayamu,
   Yasu racthum mathrum;
   Papa pari haramu,
   Yasu racthum mathrum.

4. Adi shudha chasunu,
   Yasu racthum mathrum;
   Adi shantha partsunu,
   Yasu racthum mathrum.

This language is not at all hard of acquisition, if one takes up its study in earnest and continues it a few months. By and by it will come quite easily. It usually requires a year or eighteen months to be able to discourse at length in Telugu.

During the study of the language we can do but little else. We often go out with the native preachers evenings and mornings, and though we cannot command the language to preach, it encourages the native Christians and affords the new missionary an excellent opportunity to study the people with their peculiar manners and customs. As we start out along the narrow, dirty street, the people eye us, some with amazement and some with disdain. Some respect us heartily from a sense of our personal and intellectual superiority, while others in the pride of their caste, would not come near a Christian for fear of pollution. Thirty or forty years ago, a Brahmin meeting a Christian in the road would walk a great distance around him, and if a Brahmin met a low caste native, whether Christian or not, the poor, unfortunate man must leave the road entirely, even if he had to go into a ditch or mud hole. This caste system is a most formidable thing. It is a gigantic wall of defense around Hinduism, the most troublesome barrier in the way of Christianity. It is the strongest chain with which the devil could bind a nation, and with it the Hindus have been so bound for centuries that naught but the Almighty hand

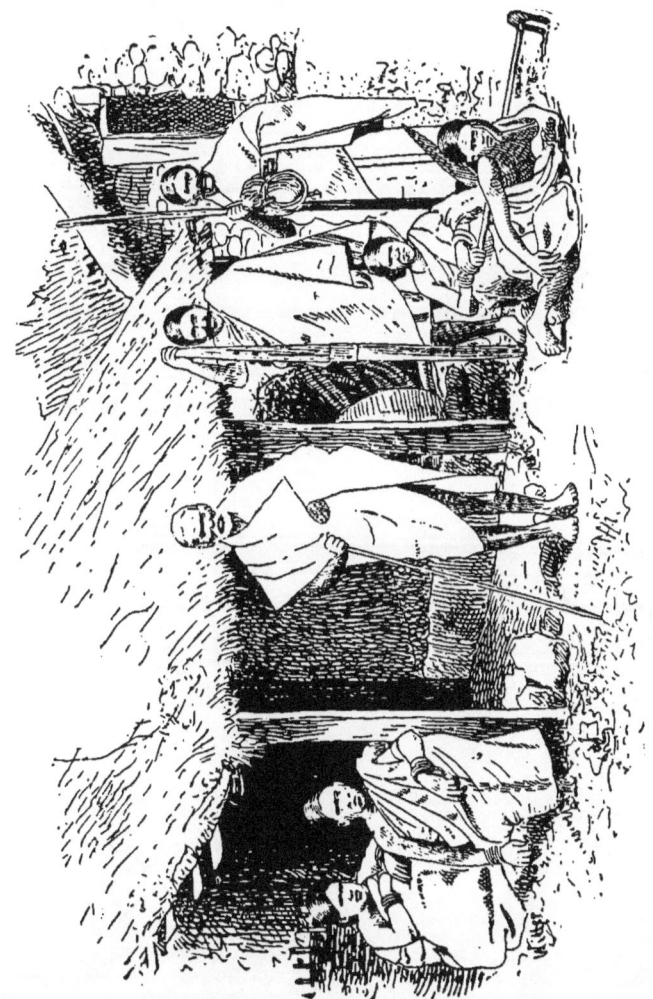

A TELUGU FAMILY.

can free them. Caste separates the people into numberless sects and classes, it precludes brotherly love; it fills all classes with prejudice which ripens into hatred one against another; it forbids progress, leads to crime and dwarfs or destroys all the finer sensibilities of the soul. So we find them at last a nation of slaves, slaves to one another and to themselves, slaves to the vile passions which rule them. There are among the Hindus four principal castes, viz.: the Brahmins, or original priests; second, the Kshetryas, or rulers; third, the Vysias, or merchantmen; and fourth, the Sudras, or laboring classes. This latter class is divided into a great number of sects, each having its name according to its occupation. Hindu law or custom forbids these casts from intermarrying, or even from eating together, and the penalty for breaking these rules is total abandonment by all the relatives, even wife and children. If a high caste man becomes a Christian, he must at once leave all his family, home and relations, go out into the world a vagabond, covered with shame and disgrace; and there is no hope for his return to his family unless they should become Christians also. It is easily seen, therefore, what it costs a Hindu to be a Christain, and what a formidable barrier is caste.

Besides the caste people, there is a fifth-class, who are considered by all others as outcasts. They are divided into two sects called Madagas and Malas. They have no caste, really, though they are full of caste pride and have but little to do with each other. Madagas are shoemakers, and Malas are weavers of coarse cloth, though now they do a great deal of farm work, since English merchandise has shortened the demand for native made goods.

The Hindu merchant sits lazily in the midst of his goods and calls out occasionally to the passers by. If you want anything and he can't reach it from his seat, he will often say he hasn't got it when you know he has, and you must insist on his getting up and looking for it. A thousand and one dirty things, fruits and sweets, are exposed for sale and for the flies. Women sit in rows along the shaded side of the streets, busily engaged in searching each others heads and when the mischievous animals are lifted, sometimes three or four at a time from the hair, they are as carefully set off on the ground as we would place a helpless babe on its bed. The Hindus never kill anything. It is contrary to their religion to take any kind of animal life. They can't kill a poisonous reptile, a scorpion, or even the smallest insect. Hence the Hindus never eat meat. They live strictly upon a vegetable diet. But the lowest classes, or outcasts, will not only eat meat, but are often the very vultures of the country, eating the loathsome carcasses found dead about the fields. This is very common, especially in famine times. There is a vast difference between classes of people. Perhaps this difference of nature and habit is the origin of caste, and then caste itself has driven the people further apart and degraded them still more. The Brahmins are a very cleanly class. They bathe their whole bodies every day, and wash and robe themselves in clean clothes very often. It can be said also to their honor that they never debase their bodies with poisonous intoxicating drinks. They are total abstainers from all intoxicants, yet the Christian (?) English are trying to impose their destroying liquors upon these better Hindus. Certainly the heathen will rise up in the day of judgment and condemn them. The lowest classes are the opposite of almost every virtue, good principle or habit. They are filthy, licentious, base in the extreme and very ignorant. I have passed by great crowds of them late in the evening, lying and sitting around the "*cullu*" (toddy) bowls. Then they often go staggering around, men and women together, quarreling, fighting, pulling hair and keeping up a general rabble until nine or ten o'clock at night, when, if they don't happen to be at home, they just tumble down most any where in a drowsy, drunken stupor, until next morning. On occasions of their annual festivities — and they are many — thousands of these people gather around the favorite idol or temple, usually in some shady grove, and there they mix with their worship, two or three nights and days of revelry in drunkenness and vice. Here is depravity unbridled. It has become so awful in some instances there has been talk of the British government prohibiting such festivals. It is a scene to make the devils blush, and a wonder that humanity could go so low. O, how greatly they need the elevating, saving power of the gospel!

An idol procession is common on all such occasions. The favorite idol is placed on a kind of frame on a two wheeled cart, the oxen dedicated to the worship of the temple, or those consecrated for the occasion, are yoked up to the cart, strung with wreaths of flowers and their regalia variously painted. The idol is usually some rude figure and near it, just in front, is a kind of receptacle or box to receive the offerings. In the van goes a native band, consisting of one to three drums and a number of pipes, horns, and the like, with which they make the music. It is a dreadful din and they seem never to weary in their ceaseless marching, piping and thumping.

Following in the rear is a great crowd of all the lower classes (the higher caste are now often ashamed to be seen in these processions), making their various offerings of rice, cocoanuts, fruits, etc., and lastly follows on a train of poor, miserable beggars, ready when the procession is over to get what has been offered to the idol. Large numbers of the poor and friendless are almost wholly supported in this way. That custom is about the only system of public charity known to the Hindus. In India, beggars, poor and helpless, are most numerous. Almost daily they come to the missionary's house, sometimes six to a dozen at once, and present themselves for assistance. If the missionary is busy, they will sit down in the yard and wait. When he comes out, or they get sight of him even through a window, they will all quickly prostrate themselves on their faces and hands, and repeat the most pitiful words in the most pitiful way they have ever learned. The missionary must go out, or they will just stay with him. Going out on the veranda, there they are; widows and orphans, old men and women, decrepit, leprous, deformed and distorted, until they scarcely resemble human beings.

Pity them; pity them! We must give them a little, yet were we to give them much, we would soon dispose of all our living.

Traveling through the streets of an average city, crowds of these unfortunate sufferers gather around us and cry for help. But there is in India another class of beggars, and sometimes it is difficult to distinguish them.

Begging is an honorable profession in India. All Brahmins are accustomed from time immemorial to make their living altogether by begging. They are ashamed of outright begging now; but there are some of the lower class who do nothing but beg. They go about in rags, assuming the air and tone of the poorest mendicant, when, in fact, they may have bags of money buried away under some rock. Missionaries in India often long for the promised land where there will be no more mosquitoes or beggars.

Hindu etiquette is rather amusing in some of its peculiarities. When a Brahmin gentleman visits a missionary, he usually sends some one ahead to announce his approach. The missionary then returns word for him to come in. As he is about to enter the door, he sees that his turban or hat is straight on his head, and carefully removes his shoes. Rather the opposite to our customs. He will then stand all the time if you do not first sit down and and tell him to be seated. Then if you rise for any cause he will also rise and remain standing so long as you are not seated. Thus regularly he will rise and sit with his host. When the host has talked with his guest for a reasonable time, and has work to do, he rises and tells his Brahmin guest he may take leave and call another time. He considers it his duty to wait for an invitation to go, and he will just stay with you if you don't tell him to go. If such were the rule of society in America, it would often be a great relief to those who have duties besides entertaining visitors. The usual method of greeting, corresponding to our "Good morning," "Good evening," etc., is to say "Salaam," and at the same time make a polite bow, touching the forehead with the inside of the open fingers of the right hand. The word salaam is used for "good morning," "good evening," "good by," and "thank you." The Hindu considers it bad etiquette to come into your presence while you are eating, and he will never put anything into his mouth while in your presence. It is customary when a white person, or native of rank, visits a high caste Hindu or Mohammedan, when the guest is about leaving, his host takes a bottle of rose water and sprinkles him well all over; sometimes if he has a wreath of flowers he hangs them around the neck of his guest. This shows his good will and a desire to honor him above the common rank of his fellows.

"The world is full of strangely acting men."

CHAPTER IV.

A HINDU WEDDING: HOT WINDS.

Before we left Ongole we had the exceptional privilege of attending a wedding among the high caste Hindus. To describe it in detail would be impossible. It required ten days to complete the ceremonies and festivities of the occasion. Imagine an American couple ten days in the marriage ceremonies; ten days, compared to two or three minutes! Some would probably dread it more than they do, and old maids and bachelors would be at a discount. Don't imagine we attended all these ten days, but only about three hours, during the principal part of the ceremonies. An old Hindu gentleman, who was in truth very favorable to Christianity, and which accounts for our presence, was having his grand-daughter, aged seven years, married to a boy ten years old. We must remember, however, that this is quite an old couple for a Hindu wedding. They are usually married between the ages of four and six. At the same time and place, this groom's father, aged forty, was married to a girl of thirteen, which was quite an unusually old age; but she was the second or third wife. So this was a double wedding. It saved time and expense; for high caste Hindu weddings are very expensive, sometimes costing as high as two thousand dollars. Bands to make music, such as it is, must be hired; dancing girls must be employed; all the relatives in the country, besides a host of Brahmins, must be fed for the whole ten days; and fruits and ornamentations by the wholesale are required. Then the parents of the bride and bridegroom must fit them up with a rich attire of silks and jewelry, amounting often to a thousand dollars worth on each one. This jewelry consists in heavy gold and silver bracelets, anklets, finger rings, toe rings, ear rings, nose rings, hair clasps and broad gold and silver belts, besides a number of silver cups. The jewelry is often the consideration of the marriage, and is henceforth kept in the family and handed down from generation to generation, and is worn and brilliantly displayed on all special occasions. When the most important of the ceremonies come, about the fifth day, the bride and groom, with all their attire of silks and jewelry, are brought out and seated under a booth, all around and above which hangs an abundance of fruit and flowers, to represent the wishes of the friends, that they may always have plenty and be ever so happy. Before them burn the candelabra of oil, and the priest takes his seat by them. He then takes a cocoanut, goes through with a number of ceremonies, chiefly in the Sanscrit language, the meaning of which he often has no idea; makes, as he supposes, a real God out of the cocoanut, lays it down and requires the couple to clasp hands and bow to it. He now lights a bundle of sticks, pours grease upon them and requires the couple to bow a number of times in worship to the fire. He then takes a piece of gold, perhaps as large as a gold dollar, pierced with a single hole, performs his munthrums over it till he is satisfied it has become a real live god. They are compelled to pay the most solemn and profound worship to this piece of gold, whereupon it becomes, henceforth, the guardian deity of their united life. They then hold out their hands toward the flame of the burning oil, and their parents, or some near relatives for them, make the most solemn vows and promises of marriage, saying them over after the priest. Some of those are in Sanscrit, and the meaning is wholly unknown to either priest or people; but they must be said. Then comes the most solemn and important part of the whole affair. The priest reverently takes this piece of deified gold, which has a string in it, hands it to the groom and instructs him to tie it around the neck of the bride. If he is too young to know how to tie it, he is assisted, and with the tying of that knot they become husband and wife. The girl becomes the property of her husband, and should he die at any time after that knot is tied, she is doomed to the fearful disgrace of a lifetime widowhood. To be a widow in India, means to be the lowest menial servant in the family, subject to the abuse of all who may meet her, and to live on the refuse of the rice bowls of others.

After this chief act of the ceremonies, all the relatives gather around and take handsful of rice and throw it over the couple, wishing them showers of blessings. It has taken two or three hours to perform these principal acts in the ceremonies, and we go home very tired of it. Then follow numberless munthrums and acts of worship, dancing and piping and drumming, eating and revelry, for nearly a week longer, until everybody is worn out and all go home. The married couple returns with their parents, as before, until the girl reaches her maturity, from twelve to fourteen, when, with some additional festivities, the young husband takes her to his own home. Then she must implicitly obey her mother-in-law as well as her husband, and the slightest transgression on her part may bring down upon herself a severe flogging. The husband considers it his duty, as well as his privilege, to whip his wife, if she displeases him in any way, and she receives it more meekly than children often receive the correction of their parents.

In India we begin to feel the heat quite sensibly in February. It increases in intensity till May, when the climax is reached. The hot winds are the dread of Europeans and natives. In April the southwest monsoon, winds sweeping up from the Indian Ocean, sets in. These winds, laden with moisture, striking the cooler tops of the western Ghauts, are condensed and fall in torrents of rain on that side of India; but long before these winds reach the eastern coast, sweeping over burning sands and under a vertical sun, they are converted into a hot steam. We have a *punkah*, or fan, made of a board a foot and a half wide and eight or ten feet long, with cloth tacked to the under edge of it, swinging from the roof by means of ropes, and kept in motion by a native outside. He draws a rope attached to the punkah and drawn through an aperture over the door. By throwing water about in the room we can keep tolerably cool. Or a better way to cool the room is to open one of the shutters toward the wind, hang up in the door a kind of coarse matting, generally made of fine grass roots, and have a native to carry water and keep it pouring on and constantly dripping down through the matting. The wind blowing through this is moistened and cooled, and the room is made quite pleasant. During this time the furniture will often dry and crack open with a report like that of a pistol. The temperature often reaches 110 to 115 degrees in the shade. The bare limbs of the natives frequently become rough and glazed over as with a hot iron. Throughout the month of May these hot winds cease not to wither and parch the green earth, and to be the bane of the inhabitants. The Telugus dread them so much that the Christians often mention among the joys of heaven, the blessed fact, that there will be no hot winds there. For the natives, however, this hot season is the healthiest. There is no malaria or poison in the air. But in June these winds give way to a heavy rainfall, usually, and the native houses being poor protection from the four or six weeks incessant rain, they take cold, are filled with malaria, and then come chills and fever with a general onslaught. Following the rain is a season of damp, sultry weather, during which time cholera often makes great ravages. The principal causes of cholera and other deadly diseases and epidemics are the great filth in all the cities and towns, poor protection from the weather, and bad or scanty food. The poor live in poorly covered mud houses, having only dirt floors. If the habits of life were in harmony with the laws of nature, the natives of India might be measurably freed from cholera and enjoy a degree of health, perhaps as good as in any other country. But the heat is so oppressive to an American that once the strength and vitality of health has given way, it is almost impossible to restore it in India.

CHAPTER V.

ACROSS THE BURNING SANDS: FAMINE, ETC.

Dr. Clough had returned to America in March, and Mr. and Mrs. Heinrichs were called to Ongole to conduct the affairs of that great mission. With those dear friends, who were at all times as our own brother and sister, the summer was spent quite pleasantly, and a fair knowledge of the language was gained. In October we were requested to go to Cumbum, a mission station sixty miles west of Ongole. To make this journey we must either take the ox cart or a four wheel conveyance drawn by men. We chose the latter for ourselves; as the weather was so hot we wanted to get through as soon as possible. Our household goods were all packed, put on carts, a few of which were sent on ahead of us, while two were left to follow. All our little necessary accompaniments were placed in the phaeton, and by the time our bedding, Mrs. Johnson, our baby and myself were all crowded in, we had quite a load. At six o'clock P. M., we rolled out of Ongole, with eight strong men as our team. We aimed to reach Cumbum by ten o'clock the next morning. But a little before daylight we missed our new set of men, who should have been waiting for us, and we were delayed three or four hours. In such travel we always get the native officer in charge of that district, to write ahead and post men for us. But we failed to find men this time. Now, the sun was rising hot upon us and we were yet thirty miles from Cumbum. Our poor little baby was nearly exhausted, and Mrs. Johnson was very tired; for neither of us had slept any during the night. We stopped and ate a little breakfast, which we had brought with us, and then had five miles to go before we could get to any place where we could be sheltered from the heat of the sun. We reached the rest house about ten o'clock and there dismissed our men, for they had drawn us already over two regular stages, and they were very tired. Here we ate the last of our food, as we aimed to have been in Cumbum by that time. But we hoped to reach Cumbum by eight or nine o'clock that night. Our supply of water was also growing low; for we must, in India, carry all our drinking water with us. We now started out with new men. Before us lay seven miles of burning sand. Had we had anything to eat and drink we would have waited till night to cross this desert. The men could not go faster than a slow walk. The sun poured down in hot fury, and the reflection and radiation from the sand were very painful. How much we all suffered I could not tell, but the worst fell upon our poor little baby, only five months old. For him we were very much alarmed. At one time there was but little hope that we could carry him across the desert alive, and, in tears, we urged the men on. But the Almighty hand that made the desert was there to comfort and strengthen. By his blessing we reached the foot of the mountain, over the plain of sand, and the evening shades brought relief from the awful heat. But now we were to confront a new trouble. It was four miles to the nearest village, and our men refused to go any farther. By paying them two days' wages, I induced two of them to go away to the village and try to get a new set of men to come and take us over the mountain. We waited there, without food or water, until late at night for their return. But, they finally returned, saying that no one would come with them. The mountain was steep and rough, and full of robbers and tigers. There we were, many miles from Cumbum, in a wild country, without food or water. The men had a few handsfull of rice, but not more than they wanted. To stay there we could only suffer. The men were about to leave us, and I could not think of leaving my wife and only child, all that was dear to me on earth, alone in such a place, to walk four miles to get men to come and take us on. We *must* go on that night. So I offered all the men double wages to take us on; but they refused. I offered them three and four times the regular wages to go on, but still they refused. It was then becoming plain to me that they realized they had me in their power, and were going to make use of their opportunity. I offered them, at last, six times the regular pay, but still they refused. I could stand it no longer. I stepped to the phaeton, and told Mrs. Johnson

MISSION BUNGALOW, CUMBUM, INDIA.

to be comforted, that we were going now, but told her nothing of the real circumstances. I then took out a lantern and my revolver and told the men to lay hold of that phaeton and start out, and not to let loose of it till I told them to. They obeyed at once, and we were soon going over the rugged mountain. I walked right by their side and watched each man. I knew it was only about five miles over the mountain, to a village where lived a number of Christians. So on we went till nearly two o'clock in the morning, when we came up to the village. God was to be praised for his deliverance. Some may be disposed to criticise my course, but I have only to say, in reply, let them be placed in similar circumstances, and see what they would do. The men were paid, at last, a little more than double wages, and they went away, apparently glad that they were so lucky. We waked some people, called for the village officer, found where the Christians were, and a number of them were glad to come to our assistance, and take us on our way. We obtained a little dirty water, and drank it at the risk of getting the cholera; for the country was full of the disease. We were tired, sleepy and hungry, almost beyond endurance, but never mind, the God of heaven was with us, and we should have plenty soon. A little after sunrise we sighted the mission house about two miles over the prairie fields. Now and then, little groves of cocoanut and palm trees, rose up in the morning light, as if to welcome us, and, ere long, we were with our friends, Mr. and Mrs. Newcomb, who had been, for eighteen hours, anxiously looking for us. And before us was spread a breakfast of plenty. "O, give thanks to the Lord; for his mercy endureth forever."

We arrived in Cumbum in the midst of a distressing famine. The monsoon rains for the two preceding years had failed of their usual quantity. No crops could be made. The poor people had nothing to eat, and no work to do. Though not so distressing as at other times, there was much suffering in the land, and some were actually starving. We went out among the villages, at one time with a government officer to investigate the condition of the people. As we passed along the road, from village to village, it was most pitiable to see the suffering people following after us. Poor women, carrying in their arms their starving little ones, running after us and begging for help, until their strength gave out. We had nothing to give them, but tried to comfort them by pointing them away from their dumb idols, to the living God, who could hear their cries. We secured an appropriation from the government for some roads and other public relief works, and on these several thousands were employed. It is a fearful religion that will allow a poor old widow to lie out in the streets and starve to death, when the wealthy have plenty in their store-houses. Yet such was the case in India. As we passed through a village, our Christians called our attention to an old woman lying on the street. We went to her and she could not raise herself up; but she made us understand that she had had nothing to eat for several days, and the merchants, who had plenty stowed away, had need to walk by her several times a day, as she lay there in her helplessness. We called some of the village officers, reproved them severely for their wickedness, and had them to get the poor woman something to eat. The reader will clearly see by this that there is not among the heathen Hindus, the first principle of charity or brotherly love. Though from unworthy motives, they occasionally help the poor. They seem more like brutes; when one is down they are only ready to gore him. O, how much they need our Savior's example of unselfish love! In famine times thousands of the poor often live for weeks on prickly pear apples, with, perhaps, some leaves gathered from the trees. These prickly pears grow very large and in great abundance in India, and, by a wise Providence, they are as plentiful in famine times as in seasons of rich harvests. If they have rice, at all, it is quite an ordinary thing, even in common seasons, for the poor to have only one meal of rice a day. They do well to have that, when we consider that they are wholly dependent on their daily wages for their living; and the common laborer's hire is from five to seven cents a day. On this pittance he must feed and clothe himself and family, however large his family may be. Their clothing, however, is not much of an item. The common laborer wears only a half yard or yard of coarse cloth tied around the body. The upper classes dress more neatly. The Brahmin wears as a lower garment, a "*puncha,*" or sort of skirt, suspended from the waist, and a "pi batta," or upper cloth, thrown loosely over the shoulders and let hang down around the body. The women of the upper classes dress very neatly. They also have a cloth gathered and hung from the waist, in the form of a neat skirt, and then a second piece is thrown over the left shoulder, crossed under the right arm, wrapped around the waist, brought over the right shoulder, crossed under the left arm, and is then often held in place by a nice silver belt. Many of the men, especially Christians, are now adopting a light sack coat for the upper garment.

Our sojourn in Cumbum was only a month. The Hanamakonda station, in the Nizam's dominions, was then vacant, and a missionary urgently needed to take up the work there. The journey was made very comfortably on the railroad. The brethren of the Deccan were in conference in Hanamakonda when we arrived. Mr. Maplesden had been in charge of the work there, but could give it only occasional visits, as his own station, eighty miles away, demanded his best attention. Our introduction to the work in Hanamakonda was very favorable. The few Christians there were very thankful that God had answered their prayers and sent them another missionary.

Our stay in Cumbum, though short, was very pleasant and profitable. Mr. and Mrs. Newcomb, are greatly loved by their people. While there, we saw much of the native character, and became better prepared for our work.

CHAPTER VI.

Origin of Idolatry: Religion of the Hindus.

Far back in the morning of history, when the human race was yet in its childhood innocency, there were none on the earth to worship idols. The living God, Creator and Father, was known of all men. But the seeds of sin were beginning to burst and put forth their buds. The enemy of the race was stealthily at work in the garden of mankind, and he was determined to seduce the human heart. The wicked seed choked out the good and brought forth its deadly fruit. Cain went forth with the seeds of depravity in him and the marks of sin upon him; with the shame of the guilty fleeing from the upright. Henceforth the race receded from the light and knowledge of God into the shades of moral and intellectual darkness. Depravity led on the downward march. Men in their sinful course thought little of God; they neglected to mention his name to their children. There was no written history of God's early dealings with man. The story of the creation, of man's sin and fall, became more and more mixed with fable and uncertainty; the outlines of true history became more and more dim, as men grew old in age and in sin; until finally truth and God were unknown, and foolish man was groping his uncertain way and chasing the phantoms of his vile passions in heathen darkness. There are to-day many traces among heathen races of this downward course; milestones marking the stages, one by one, as man went down. Among nations where the Bible has not been heard of, are mythical stories of the creation and fall of man, bearing a semblance to that of the Bible; among the followers of Confucius, Buddha and Brahma are the faint echoes of ancient prophecy of a great one rising up by divine power to deliver his people. This old Bible idea of a Savior has taken on different forms as it went on further into the darkness of heathendom. There are many traces of it to be found in nearly every heathen creed; but they bear upon their faces the marks of inconsistent fable, and stand as proofs to the intelligent that the Bible record is the only true one and they are but the shadows, or distant and indistinct echoes of the original, floating along down through the dark ages until the dull ears of men could no longer understand; but their depraved imagination caught up the blank and filled it out as they chose. They changed the image of the incorruptible into corruption itself. Sin led on to sin, until the father of sin possessed the kingdom. Millions of the human race now in total forgetfulness of God, must worship something, and so make them gods after their own likeness. O, how fallen! Man was created in the image of God; but now depraved man is making gods in his own image.

How kindred is this human spirit to that which in open rebellion sought to displace the Almighty from his throne and set himself up instead! Seeing this near kinship, we may say, with sorrowful solicitude, of all idol worshipers, "Ye are of your father, the devil." Men, by their own actions, locate themselves. They bear the likeness of their father. Poor fallen man must worship, and if he doesn't know the true God, the devil is always there to claim his devotion. Thus millions of our fellow men fall down before demons and devils, and know it not. Proud men in our own country know of God and the devil both and choose themselves in preference to either; yet the heathen knows better than to worship himself.

In ignorance of God, the worship of some was directed toward the sun. This great giver of light and heat was seen to have so much influence over all the earth, insomuch that all animal and vegetable life was dependant on him; the people knew not to look beyond the creature to the Creator, but supposed the sun to be god and worshipped it. There are to-day many sun-worshippers. In the same way they believed the moon, planets and stars to be smaller gods, and worshipped them. There is a tradition among some that the sun is the father of the divine family, the moon the wife, and the stars the children. So when they see a shooting or falling star they say it is one of the children being cast out for his wickedness. Seeing that wind, fire and water hold or exert a mystic or incomprehensible power, men, in their moral darkness, concluded that these elements were possessed of divinity, and worshipped them. The Parsees are devoted fire-worshippers to this day, and the Hindus are more or less worshippers of fire. The most sacred oath or obligation a Hindu can take is performed over fire. At this stage of sin, ignorance and darkness, into which a great portion of mankind had degenerated, we open the first pages of Hindu history. We here find them with a religion called Vedism or worship of the elements. The Vedas, the oldest sacred books of the Hindus, is a collection of songs and prayers addressed to these different elements in nature.

But by and by there seemed to occur a sort of reform, and Vedism gave way to Brahminism. Brahminism is one step higher. It looks beyond the mere elements and conceives of a general agency or power, a supreme motor that keeps the machinery of nature in motion, and names this power, whatever it may be, Brahma. Brahma, then, becomes the supreme god and claims the highest worship. But Brahminism in its purity was not long the common faith. Here man makes a blunder too common to all classes and nations. He begins to reason from self outward and says that Brahma can not be alone as the only inhabitant of the realm of diety, and so he must have companions to break the cheerless solitude. Now come two other gods, and we have the Brahmin triad: Brahma, Vishnu and Siva. Brahma, the creator; Vishnu, the preserver, and Siva, the destroyer. But passionate man could not be satisfied with three gods. Like men, they must have wives. So wives they created for their gods, and as they do yet, the priests performed the wedding ceremonies. Then there must be more gods and goddesses. Any number were created; one to preside over every distinct feature of nature, one for the giving of every separate blessing to man. Then there must be evil as well as good ones, and so a great number of bad gods were created and *they* must have wives; so the manufacture of gods and goddesses goes on, *ad infinitum*, until in the laws of Manu, an old Hindu sage, we have enumerated no less than three hundred and thirty millions of gods and goddesses. Wonderful! India, with more gods than people; a land overflowing with gods, and yet so godless!

This is Hinduism. "Hinduism," as said by another, "is Brahminism gone to seed." Hinduism is the present religion of the masses of the people of India. It is gross idolatry. Every man has his idol; almost everything is an idol. Nearly everything in nature is worshipped—animal and vegetable. The sacred bull is a special object of worship, and all cows are looked upon as sacred beings, insomuch that the people take the excrement of the cow, make a very thin paste and cover the walls of their houses with it to purify the air and keep away disease. The cow is worshipped devoutly by many. All the meanest animals are worshipped, even the deadliest serpents.

The cobra is the worst snake in India, as it is the most vicious and deadly poison. No cure is known for its bite, and its victim usually dies in a few minutes. It will attack any one who disturbs it. They are numerous, also, but not very large, their length being usually from four to five feet. The poor natives, always afraid of being bitten by them, go to their holes with cocoanut milk and rice, pour them down into their holes and offer prayer to the cobra, beseeching it not to bite them or any of their family. Their religion teaches them that it is murder to kill any animal; hence no snakes, scorpions, or other dangerous animals, are ever killed. It would, in fact, in the eyes of some Hindus, be a greater sin to kill a cow than to kill a woman. For, in truth, a woman is about the only thing in creation that a Hindu will not worship.

Because of this fault of religion, India is full of all kinds of dangerous wild animals, reptiles and insects. It has been estimated that in India twenty-five thousand persons are destroyed annually by snakes and wild beasts. The Bengal tiger is the dread of the country. Not a man, woman, or child, who does not dread the name of a tiger.

Panthers, leopards and bears are quite numerous. The Mohammedans are the only class who would kill any thing, and they have never had sufficient firearms to cope with these larger animals. The religion of the people destroys its own subjects, both soul and body. Of course the high caste Hindus never eat meat of any kind, and the missionary in India, if he has any meat, must obtain a little mutton or chicken from the Mohammedans. The Hindus believe also in the transmigration of souls, but not to the extent Buddhists do. This belief accounts, in part, for their indisposition to take animal life; for in killing a dog, they might be guilty of murdering an uncle or grandfather. Their souls are said to be born again into higher or lower animals, according as they have been good or bad. If bad, they will, next-birth enter into the cattle herd; if bad there, they will next time, perhaps, be a dog; if a bad dog, they may next time be a snake, and so on down to the lowest insect. But if a good man he will next be a wealthy officer; if still good, next time he will be a king, and if a good king, he will then enter the realm of inferior deity; then a superior god, and finally, according to the Buddhist theory, if he holds out faithful, he reaches the blest Nirvana, or the state of annihilation. After he reaches that state, there is no more fear of his ever becoming degenerated into a lower being.

That is the highest happiness, and the most inspiring hope this poor religion has to offer to suffering mankind. How dark! The mere hope that after thousands and perhaps millions of years of perseverance in good works and self torture, the poor soul may have the bliss of going out of existence as a safeguard against further evil! But the Christian, after a few years of conflict with sin and sorrow, during which time he has the support and comfort of the unseen but ever present Spirit, leans confidently, in the hour of death, on a merciful and forgiving Savior, and with him at last, enters into mansions of resplendent glory; there to be at home forever! Joy, bliss, and endless praise!! O, how different! How much these people need Christ! Dear reader, could you go and make Him known to them?

On every hill top, under every green tree, their temples and pagodas stand. Crowds of people may be seen in the early morning making their way out from the villages, gathering around the public wells for the purification baths. These are taken by pouring water over their bodies out of earthen pots; and then in their blindness, they gather around the temples. The larger temples have an inner small chamber where the idols are kept; then an inner and an outer wall. There will be, perhaps, a very large idol to which the temple is dedicated; then, associated with it, a number of smaller ones. The worshippers enter the gate of the outer wall, approach the inner gate, confront the idols, and then with clasped hands, bow to the earth, calling on the name of the idol. Rising, they walk slowly around the temple, until they reach the same front again, when they repeat their worship. Depending on the nature of their troubles, they may keep up this process of worship from one hour to all day. Mothers carrying their children around the temples, teaching the helpless innocents to fall down before an ugly block of stone.

The Hindus have only two reasons for their worship. First, because they are in need and want something; and, second, because they fear some approaching danger or disease. To obtain the one and keep away the other is the object of all their worship. How different from the Christian's worship! As well as trusting God for those things which we daily need, and to protect us from all evil, we worship our God because he is our Creator. Legions of angels cease not neither day nor night to worship Him, and, should not mortal man, in spirit and truth, worship God? We worship Him because he has shown us such depths of love. He has in great mercy prepared for us a way of eternal salvation, salvation through a wonderful sacrifice, which He himself has laid on the altar for us. Shall we not lay upon the altar of His worship the deepest affections of our hearts? O, we look into the love-beaming face of a Christ who saves us; and we worship! We look confidently on to the blissful home of the soul which he has prepared for us and we worship. But the heathen, in his distressing need, goes out to his dumb idol; he stares famine or disease in the face, and tremblingly turns to the cold stone for protection. With a dreadful sense of guilt and foreboding of a dark and awful future, he flees to the dead image that mockingly, only echoes his cries. And when his body is tired, he returns to his lonely hovel more distressed and shrouded in darkness than ever before. Yes, "Why do the heathen rage, and the people imagine a vain thing?" The heathen beclouded in spiritual darkness, convinced of the vanity and folly of his worship, sits down in dispair to die, and be numbered with his forefathers. Lost! LOST!! LOST!!!

> O, sad and awful death!
> No hope of God; beneath the sod,
> His mortal body lies.
> No hope of heav'n, no sins forgiv'n;
> So with his dying breath,
> To sink to hell, and there to dwell,
> In endless pain and sighs.

Rarely do we find in India a man who, feeling the burden of sin, desires inward peace and seeks relief of his gods. But one notable case of this kind deserves special mention. He was a rajah, or king, of a small district lying northwest of Ongole. During a great many years he had made many pilgrimages to the noted shrines of India, and each time was only the more burdened. He tortured himself and suffered many privations in his fruitless endeavors to obtain that peace for which the soul was longing. And when at last, he heard Dr. Clough preaching Jesus as the healing balm of the soul, he clapped his hands and shouted before all the people, "Praise to the God of peace! Jesus, the Savior! That is what I have been hunting for for fifty years, and found it not till this happy day!" So he embraced Jesus as his Savior, and from that time till his death, ceased not to preach that gospel which was indeed to him such good tidings of great joy.

The heathen in their worship are very devoted, if they are in trouble or in great need. During the famine in and around Cumbum, in 1891, the people were daily around the temples, and carrying their chief idols in triumphal processions up and down the streets. The Christians told us an amusing story which will illustrate the extreme of heathen folly. After several weeks of fruitless efforts to induce their gods to send rain on the parched earth, they became enraged and declared if the gods would not be persuaded by kindness, they would compel them to grant their desires. So they took them out of the temples, and abusing their majesty most terribly, threw them down into a ditch, and pelted them most furiously with clods of dirt; saying to them, that may be next time they would pay more attention to their prayers and send rain and plenty in the land.

TEMPLE OF A THOUSAND PILLARS, HANAMAKONDA, INDIA.

CHAPTER VII.

Degeneration, the Fruit of Idolatry.

Looking over the moral condition of India, we are reminded of an old field which has been neglected for a great many years, and is now grown up with great wild weeds, briers and bushes, and having an occasional old burnt tree stretching forth its bare limbs into the sighing winds. Blossoms and fruit are all gone, and in their places stand the wild, rank growth of a depraved soil.

What may have been the former condition of India, we cannot tell; but there is abundant evidence of an ancient civilization much higher than anything now found among the Hindus. In many parts of India are now to be found massive ruins of old temples, and pieces of statuary, rivaling in taste and beauty of sculpture anything produced in modern times. There are, in Hanamakonda, the ruins of a once magnificent temple, having originally a thousand pillars. The most of it is of black marble, and the excellence of art thereon displayed is truly wonderful. In other places in India there are beautiful palatial temples, all cut out of the solid rock of the mountain side. These things all speak silently, but distinctly, of a lost art, of a civilization somewhere buried in the decline of the past. Despite the evolutionist theory, the masses of the human race have gone down rather than up, and in place of a constant development, degeneration and decline mark every page of human history. Only a small portion of the race has escaped this dark and downward current, and has only by the light of the Bible risen to the eminence of which we boast. From the Jewish race, and their scriptures, a small, but constant stream of light has shown along down the ante-christian ages. Then, the great light, which blazed out over Syria, lit up, for a while, nearly every nation of the Levant, and all the East felt it. But men, because their deeds were evil, loved darkness rather than light, and so closed their eyes to its radiant beams, until it almost ceased to shine in their borders. Then all along through the dark ages, like stars through the midnight clouds, burst out only occasional flashes of pure light. Densest darkness brooded over the entire earth; and in that darkness, though somewhat broken, still grope the most of mankind. Man, in his wickedness, forgot God, who alone could hold him up. He neglected to live by the principles of righteousness, but was led off by his own lusts. They led him, as they will lead any one, to moral death. Depraved mankind is floating in an ocean of sin, and if he doesn't want to sink, he had better not let loose of God; for he alone can hold him up and save him. But the early families of the race did let loose of Him, and forgot Him. Then, in the ocean of sin, they gave way to human passion; because, first intoxicated, they then reveled in sin, and last of all, went down in the vortex of moral ruin. It is a sad picture. O, why will men forget their God, their only possible life and support?

It is a principle in moral science, which we should all, and always remember, that for immortal man, the first step downward is to forget God. Then follows sin upon sin; sin degrades the moral nature, and leads to further and greater sins. The man then goes on like a railway car turned loose upon a great down grade, onward the soul sweeps, rushing to destruction, until it lands, at last, in hell, the only terminus of that moral down-grade. Think of it; at every alternate tick of the clock, some immortal soul is landed into that dreadful terminus! Two hundred and fifty millions in India, two hundred millions in Africa, three hundred and fifty millions in China, are steadily moving on, tramp, tramp, tramp, along their death march, to the regions of the lost. They had forgotten God; the devil did not forget them, and they are brought low. The moral nature becoming so degraded, the mental, also, as a natural result, must follow in the same decline. Hard upon moral and mental degradation follows, by natural law, the degeneration of the physical man. All this is but natural, and verified too often, in our own country, as well as among heathen tribes. In heathen lands, how solemn and sad the spectacle! Millions of our fellow beings, so awfully abased in soul, mind and body. Their religion, led on by innate depravity, has done it all. A man's religion makes him what he is. The religion of a nation, or people, determines the character of that people or nation. Mankind is now divided into three classes, viz.: those who have a good religion; second, those who have a bad religion, and, third, those who have no religion at all. The only true and good religion is that which comes from a perfect God, the fountain head of all truth, wisdom and righteousness; and so, by this religion, men are continually lifted up, enriched with the truth, endowed with wisdom, and filled with righteousness. All bad religions are traps set for the destruction of man, and, being from the devil, the fountain head of all lies, vice and moral darkness; those, who cling to such a religion, never come to the truth, are filled with vice and shame, and in ignorance and moral darkness, are bound to destruction by the chain which they have forged, sunken down in the pit which they made.

Of all monstrosities in the human family, the man who denies all religion is certainly the most extravagant. He worships no God but himself, and finds, in all the religions of the world, no wisdom like his own. With no hope to offer his fellow man who naturally looks to a God to control his future, he lives in and for himself, and dies, at last, like the man who was drowned trying to walk the Red Sea in cork boots. He lost his equilibrium, his head went under, and nothing could be seen but his inverted boots. Poor man that will set himself up against nature and against God! O, that all mankind knew and loved the God who can save them. Eight hundred millions of our race, so poisoned by that spiritual malaria, so sick with sin, subversive malady, dropping one by one into graves of despair! Fathers taking their sons by the hand and leaping in the darkness to awful ruin; mothers, clinging to their offspring, go down with them to a common fate.

> O, how it moves the Christian heart
> To see his fellow man go down
> In dark despair to take his part
> With those beneath God's righteous frown.
>
> We weep, and cannot reach them now,
> But, O, the hope lights up the soul,
> I'll go and teach the children how
> To gain the Christian's blessed goal.

And coming generations may,
In Christian love and gratitude,
Rise up to bless the happy day,
They learned that sweet beatitude.

All the vicious and intemperate habits of the Hindus are largely due to the teachings of their religion. The nonprogressive spirit of the people of India is but the inculcation of ancient Vedism. The Vedas taught that in the beginning the gods created and placed before man everything he needed, and that to attempt improvement of any kind would be an insult to deity. Accordingly all inventions and improvements are shut off from the race, and, today, the farmers, the mechanics, the tradesmen, walk in the same footprints their forefathers made four thousand years ago. In all moral questions, however, as it is impossible for a people to remain on the same level, they have gone down. Among the worst fruits of an idolatrous religion may be mentioned

The Universal Degradation of Woman. It is so in all heathen lands. Wherever the Bible is not known the dignity and rights of woman are not respected. Christianity and an elevated womanhood go hand in hand. He that was born of the sweet virgin was the first to lift womanhood from the thraldom of slavery. Wherever, among the families of the earth, His religion sways the moral powers, softens and purifies the affections, men acknowledge and respect the worth of a true woman.

In India, it is a sad misfortune to be a woman. We have already mentioned the disconsolate state of widowhood. The birth of a girl baby is a bad omen, a token of evil, and everybody goes about with a gloomy countenance. The poor mother weeps over her misfortune and patiently bears the abuse of her husband.

Some better idea may be obtained from an incident in the experience of one of our lady missionaries. She, being a doctor, was called to see a native woman who was thought to be dying. After giving the necessary attention to the woman, she asked where her baby was. A dirty, impudent little man, sitting lazily on the floor in the corner of the room, pointed outside. She went out, and under a buffalo shed, on the bare ground, lay a poor little infant starving to death; so near gone it was unable to make a noise. The missionary was filled with pity and indignation. She returned into the house and asked what was meant by such conduct; whereupon the cool reply: "O, never mind that; it's only a girl." If a boy baby is born the mother rejoices, the husband honors and compliments her, and all the relatives hold a jubilee. Thanks and propitiatory offerings are made to the patron god, and all the people look forward to good times.

The women of the higher classes after they go to their husbands' houses, are kept confined within zenana walls for the rest of their days. The zenana is much like a convent, being inclosed in high walls. It usually has a number of separate buildings. Some of the rooms are for the men and some for the women. If, for any cause, they are compelled to go outside of these walls, they must go under cover and must neither see or be seen. In the zenanas no man but the husband, father or brother is ever admitted to the presence of the women. The origin of this ridiculous practice of keeping the women imprisoned, dates back, perhaps, to the time when war and rapine was the rule and no man's life or property was safe. In such times the rulers were accustomed to seize any woman to whom they happened to take a fancy and without any regard, carry her away from her husband. Consequently all beautiful women were guarded with the most jealous care; and so they are today, as the people never consider it worth their while to change their customs to suit the times in which they live.

The women must do all the menial work; they must gather the buffalo chips for cooking, must prepare the food and serve while the men and boys eat. It is the custom among all classes for the men and boys to be seated all on the floor. They have no chairs, tables, dishes, knives or forks. Each has an earthen bowl or dish before him; the woman brings out the pot of rice and with her hand serves them all around. Then she either retires from the room, or fans her husband while he eats. They all dip into the rice with their hands, cram their mouths as full as possible, let the rest fall back into the bowl and then bring up another handful. After the men and boys are well filled the women and girls may take what is left.

The women of the lower classes have this advantage over the high caste women, that they work for wages and so have liberty to go wherever they please. How much the women of India need the tender hand of the divine Son of Mary to lift them out of slavery and disgrace.

It is the special work of many of our lady missionaries to visit the women confined in these zenana prisons and there preach to them the Gospel; for ladies only may ever see them, and but for such work, these women could never see a Gospel witness nor ever hear the words of life. Hearing, some of them believe.

CHAPTER VIII.

PERSECUTION: MOHAMMEDANISM.

Persecution in India is not what it once was, and now is in other heathen lands.

The country being under British rule, missionaries are well protected from violence, and their rights are respected by all the natives. In fact there is, perhaps, no heathen country in any other part of the world where the missionary is so well protected as in India. The natives must respect the European officer and the masses know no difference between white people, missionaries, or officers. Often the poor, when they want a favor, come to the missionary and almost worship him. It is a common thing when a British officer passes through the streets of a village to see great numbers of natives prostrating themselves before him. They are a helpless people and so depend like children upon their superiors for a support. They are all well educated in the art of flattery. They have learned this art from the old courts of autocrats. They were accustomed to grant favors to their vassal subjects for pleasing flattery. The poor when seeking favors were in the habit of coming into the presence of the rulers and in great swelling words reciting their beauty, greatness and glory; when the conceited autocrat, pleased with himself, would grant the request of his worshipper.

This system of flattery is soon introduced to the missionary on his arrival in India. In his presence, they are astonished at his magnificent appearance, his profound learning, and his wonderful devotion and self-sacrifice. But among his own people that Hindu has not enough bad words with which to abuse the missionary. Notwithstanding all his flattery and persistent show of friendship, the Hindu is to be watched. Feigning the greatest love, several attempts have been made on the lives of missionaries. Murder is not a common thing among Hindus, but the method generally adopted is by poisoning. Once a great number of people brought some fine mango fruit to a missionary. It was delivered with a great pompous speech, setting forth the common brotherhood between the Hindu and the American. Though the mangoes were received with thanks, they were carefully set away till next morning, when on examination the largest and most inviting one was found to be saturated with poison and perfectly black.

The Hindus are persistent in their efforts to oppose Christianity. They have, in Madras and other large cities, organized societies for the production and distribution of Hindu anti-Christian literature. They resort to various methods. If they find any one studying Christianity they begin immediately to prejudice them, and to remove all impressions that may have been made by the Gospel.

They follow up the missionary with their pernicious system of ridicule. They revive and preach their own religion when they see it about to die in the heart of a subject. Once, when we went on a tour, a high caste man was very favorably disposed toward Christianity and said if his wife would follow him he would become a Christian. The next morning all her relatives gathered around, bringing their cocoanut milk and rice and proposed a visit to the cobra snake hole. They worship these snakes very devotedly. They took this man's wife, he being too intelligent to take any part in such foolish worship, and away they went on their pilgrimage to the snake hole. They thus led her off and away from the probability of hearing the Gospel and hoped we might be gone ere they returned. They pour the milk and rice into the hole, hoping that the snake will receive it and be so much pleased thereby that it may never be disposed to bite them or any of their relatives.

When the missionary preaches, the old priest will come and stand around, watching to see what effect the Gospel is having on his people. If he sees any impression is made he seeks to counteract it. The priest endeavors to frighten the poor people, making them believe if they forsake their ancestral religion, all the gods and goddesses of their forefathers will turn loose their fury upon them. They seek to weaken the faith of the Christians and intimidate them by threatening them with the curse of the gods. If they have any misfortune, the heathen declare it is because the gods are angry with them. If they have more blessings than the heathen—and they usually have—they take the curious alternative of saying the Christians have deceived the gods. The Brahmin watches, with jealous care, every movement of the missionary.

But the greatest hindrance to the progress of Christianity is that great citadel of heathenism—caste. Men are bound by it; they are imprisoned and safely guarded by it. We have already mentioned how difficult it is for one to break the environments of caste and ever again enjoy the company of his family.

All these things work against the progress of the Gospel among the Hindus; but the most virulent opposition is by

The Mohammedans.—They comprise about one-sixth of the population of India. The country was once conquered and ruled, for a long time, by the Mohammedans. They, as well as the Jews, are a peculiar people. The pure blooded Mohammedans are descended directly from Ishmael; and there is an interesting relation between the descendants of those half brothers, Isaac and Ishmael. Both, in their places, fulfilled the great purposes of God; for he promised Hagar, to make of her son a great nation, and covenanted with Abraham that Isaac should stand at the head of a host who should number as the stars of heaven or the sands of the sea shore. Both promises are being fulfilled. Yet the jealousy which sprang up between Hagar and Sarah, more than thirty-seven centuries ago, still burns between the children of their sons. God said to Abraham that the children of his son Isaac should possess the gates of their enemies. Who are, to them, greater enemies to-day than their Saracen cousins? This prophecy, at least, suggests the probable destiny of that warlike and blood-thirsty race. They are to-day the most unscrupulous, uncompromising enemies of the seed of Isaac, and of all those who have been blessed in his seed according to the promise. The Mohammedans have their origin, as such, from Mohammed, a man of unusual talent and boldness. He rose to eminence in the early part of the Seventh Century. He was born in Mecca, Arabia; but when he pressed his claims as a prophet upon the people of his own town they drove him out as an impostor. He fled from Mecca to Medina, where he remained till he obtained a sufficient following to take up the sword against his enemies. He then, professing to have had in a vision such orders from heaven, called his faithful together, told them that God Almighty had ordered them to conquer the world to his teaching, and for their own zeal to reap the spoil of the conquest. They must spare none, but compel all to acknowledge God, and Mohammed as his chief prophet. The proposition was favorable to human pride and ambition, and with Mohammed in the lead they set out for Mecca. Entering the town of his birth, he compelled every inhabitant, at the point of the sword, to acknowledge him as God's prophet. Then, to strengthen his force, he offered all men who would join his army and fight for him, pardon, protection of life and property, and to share also in the spoils of battle. It was an easy matter among such people to soon have an immense army at his back. He then proceeded to subdue all Arabia, and was planning for the conquest of the whole world, when his victorious career was suddenly cut short by death. But his followers grasped the opportunity and took up the sword he had laid down. They proceeded in every direction, laying everything at their feet, till the north, east, west and south bowed beneath the crescent. Sweeping around the northern coast of Africa, they crossed the Straits of Gibraltar and proceeded over the Pyrenees into Europe; but here, in the battle of Tours, they were, for the first time, defeated and driven back.

Thinking over what might have been, we have to thank the God of the nations for their defeat in that battle; for, had the Saracen conquerors been permitted to advance into Europe, we all might to-day have been Mohammedans, and, instead of the glorious stars and stripes, lit up by the splendor of a free and Christian land, over our capitol might wave the flag of a foreign despot.

The sword was everywhere the effectual means of conversion. Wherever they compelled the people to accept the Koran, it was taught to their children, and they believed it, and so, in one or two generations, millions of people were firm believers in Mohammed. That same warlike spirit and murderous character which, in their conquest, was everywhere exhibited, is still the characteristic of every Mohammedan, and had they the power, the life of a Christian would be nothing in their hands. Their deadly hatred toward Christians may be seen in the following. They have a custom that if a Mohammedan accidently kills one of his own people, he may atone for the sin, both for time and eternity, by killing four Christians. The Mohammedans are especially bitter against one of their own number who becomes a Christian. Consequently there are, in India, but very few converts from among the Mohammedans. It seems not to be God's time for their redemption. The door to that peculiar people is still closed; when, if ever, it may be opened, the God of the nations only knows. In India, one of the principal centers of Mohammedanism is Hyderabad, the capital of the Nizam's dominions. The Nizam is a

Mohammedan tributary ruler. He governs his own country and people, insofar as he doesn't do anything to conflict with British laws as applied to native states. He is compelled to support, in the midst of his territory, a standing army of British soldiers. This army serves the double purpose of protecting the Nizam from his enemies, and of making him and his people behave themselves. Every year this army has a grand parade, and his highness, the Nizam, has to come out and make his bow to the British flag. The city of Hyderabad, in which the Nizam lives, lies four square, and is inclosed by a great wall with four entrance gates. The city, inside, is divided into regular geometrical squares. The inhabitants, who always live within the walls, are said to be Arabs of the most savage and blood-thirsty character. Several years ago it was quite unsafe for any but Mohammedans to enter the city, and but few will enter it now without great precaution. These Arabs are always armed with knives and swords and, if they choose, may run up and thrust a knife or sword through a victim and retreat into the buildings in any direction, where they are all agreed, and he is received with honor if he has killed a Christian, and there he is beyond the reach of justice. The whole city, two hundred thousand or more, must be implicated to get one man. Europeans, if they enter the city now, usually have a guard with them, or drive through in closed carriages. It is not considered safe to stop in the streets though, as British influence is more and more felt among them, the danger of entering the city is less. The Nizam is a profligate; though they claim a Mohammedan must not touch intoxicating drinks. He is said to be almost always drunk. He has about one hundred and fifty wives. As he is seldom fit for business, his prime minister is really the ruler. He is very fond of tiger hunting; and goes out every year to his tiger reservation, in which no one else is allowed to hunt, and shoots tigers. As the Hindus never kill anything, and but few Mohammedans have sufficent guns for tigers, they have multiplied to great numbers. But tiger hunting is very dangerous and his highness is not disposed to take any risk. So he has a very high scaffold prepared near a path leading out of a jungle to some watering place. He comes in on his elephant, takes a comfortable seat on this scaffold and then sends in a great company of his poor subjects, with drums and tom-toms, to frighten out the tigers. Hearing the terrible din all around him, the tiger leaves his den and makes for the watering place. While he thus passes the Nizam has nothing to do but shoot him. Some hunt tigers on elephants; but that is not always safe. Others, lovers of danger, go on foot among them and risk their lives on the certainty of their shot. In our own station are the graves of two British officers who lost their lives in such daring attempts. In meeting and shooting at a tiger it is almost inevitable death to the hunter if his aim is not certain and his shot deadly. We have been told by old hunters that men have been torn to pieces, even after their shot had penetrated the heart of the tiger, so fierce and rapid are they in their actions. The safest shot is to break their neck, when, of course, they are helpless. We never had any ambition for tiger hunting.

Is it not a pity that any religion will not

only refuse to destroy such beasts but teach the people to worship them? Yet such is the faith of the Hindus.

The Mohammedans seeing the progress of the Christian cause, have organized against it. In Hyderabad city, among the nobles of the court, where money is no object and hatred toward the Bible is the rule, there is a society for the propagation of Islam and the opposition of missionary effort. They employ their preachers, as we do, and send them out to every station where there is a Christian missionary. Like hounds they follow after us day by day. If we go out to a distant village, the next day, or close on our tracks, comes the Mohammedan preacher seeking to counteract all we may have done. He does but little preaching of his own religion; but ceases not with all the vile epithets at his command to abuse and belie the missionary, ridicule the Bible and blaspheme the name of Christ. Daily he walks the streets, gathers the people around him and pours out among them his vile calumny. The Mohammedans everywhere seek to prejudice the minds of the people against the missionary. If they can't do it by ridicule and falsehood, they threaten the people. In the Nizam's dominions nearly all the government officers are Mohammedans, and the life and property of the poor are in their hands. If they see in the people any disposition to consider the claims of the Gospel, they threaten to cut off their support, to beat them and to take away their property. Thus intimidated, the poor people are afraid to be seen near a missionary or native preacher.

Once during a great annual feast in Hanamakonda, nine or ten men and women from a village thirty miles away, had come on a pilgrimage to the temple. While on the streets they for the first time heard the Mohammedans abusing the missionary and his religion. It was all a new thing to these simple but earnest people, and they expressed a desire to see that "foreign deceiver," as he was called, and hear what that religion was which brought down upon itself so much abuse.

The Mohammedans told them that if they entered the mission yard they would beat them all so that they could not get home. But their curiosity was all the more aroused, and they determined to see the missionary at all hazards, but said no more about it. The next morning our bell rang for service, and they came and took their seats in the yard just in front of the chapel door. They were afraid to go in, but they must hear what was said by the preacher. After our service was closed and most of the people gone, we went out to them. They were loath to leave; they wanted to hear more about that wonderful Savior. Then for more than an hour, we preached Christ to them and, as we closed our talk, more than half of them rose up and said, "We know that what you say must be true, and we believe it. It is so wonderful." So the work of the devil was turned to the glory of God. On another occasion the Mohammedan preacher was in a little village near Hanamakonda, profaning the Bible and the name of Christ. A great many of the people, when he left, determined to hear more about Christ. They had been preached to a number of times, but were now excited to greater interest.

Sunday came and our deep-toned bell invited all to come to the house of God. Twelve of the leading men came. They walked in and took their seats on the chapel floor, as is the custom. We appointed one of our native evangelists, who happened to be present that morning, to sit down with them and instruct them in the Bible, while we went on with the Sunday-school lesson. The spirit of God seemed to be present in unusual power. We all felt the solemnity of the hour. The time came on for the sermon and we turned it to a prayer meeting. We besought God to save those twelve men; they were convicted and fell on their faces in prayer. Soon they began to rise up and confess Christ until the last of the twelve shouted, "O, yes, I know Jesus will save us all; praise his name." That day His name was honored in Hanamakonda. The twelve were received immediately into the church, and at the close of the service we led nine of them into the liquid grave, and before all that heathen throng they were buried with Christ in baptism, and rose again to walk in newness of life. Truly was it that day fulfilled, "He that sitteth in the heavens shall laugh; the Lord shall have them in derision." For the heathen lookers-on were that day ashamed and without an answer.

In His name why not all Christians accept the promise: "Ask of me and I will give thee the heathen for thine inheritance and the uttermost parts of the earth for thy possession," and so shall it be. The devil may rage, the kings of the earth may set themselves together, and the rulers take counsel against the Anointed; but to its uttermost parts, the world shall be full of his knowledge and glory as the waters cover the sea.

CHAPTER IX.

The Telugu Mission: Its Beginning and Struggles.

After seeing so much of the people, their life and condition, the reader will be anxious to know what has been done for their relief. During the last century there has been such an awakening among Christian people of every nation; money has been consecrated; missionaries have been sent out to evangelize the world, and the voice of God has sounded in the heart of every continent. How have the millions of India shared in the blessing? The story of missions in India is absorbingly interesting and, in the eyes of all the world, truly wonderful. I need not here recount the lives and work of Judson, Carey and others; it is all familiar to those much interested in missions. But the influence of their devoted lives is felt in every department of the work. Their labors have contributed to the success of all missionary enterprise since their day. The pathetic story of self-sacrifice, of persecutions, imprisonment, of suffering under the tropical sun, of bleeding feet over the burning sands and rocks, deeply thrills the soul of every missionary, urging him to do and dare for the master. A visit to Serampore brings up the labors of those men of God, who, through the press, opened up to so many millions the Gospel. The missionary looks out upon the bay of Bengal, remembers what Judson did and endured for Jesus, think how, in the absence of his loved ones, he was buried at last in those deep waters; and there seems to come a spirit and a whisper up from the sea saying, "Be ye faithful unto death." The graves of others, where the leopard and the tiger leap, and the winds sigh in the lone palms, all speak to the living and urge them on to nobler deeds. Since the days of Carey and Judson, heroic spirits have not been wanting. Hundreds of men and women now on the field are ready, when it becomes necessary, to suffer even unto death for Christ's sake. Through their labors, since the days of these first noble heroes, many thousands have been led to Christ. Others have taken up the work which they laid down and carried it on to sublimer results than their brightest hope ever pictured.

Much has been done in the north of India by the English Baptists, Methodists and others; but the work of the American Baptist Missionary Union among the Telugus has been the greatest, and shall occupy our chief attention. The mission to the Telugus was begun in 1836, when Rev. Samuel S. Day arrived among them. He labored in Vizagapatam, Chicacole and Madras; but early in 1840 he went to Nellore and there founded the first mission station. Owing to the scarcity of Telugu books, the language was difficult of acquisition, and various other serious difficulties confronted him in his pioneer work. Touring throughout the country and preaching the Gospel to all classes, he labored for nearly two years, when he had the privilege of baptising the first Telugu convert. Dr. Downie, in his history of the Telugu mission, gives an account of this interesting occasion. "Towards sunset on the 27th day of September, 1841, a little company might have been seen wending its way towards the Pennar river. Right under the shadow of the great Nellore temple, on the river bank, they sang a hymn; the missionary read a few passages of Scripture and explained the nature of the ordinance about to be celebrated. By this time a large crowd of natives had assembled and Mr. Day embraced the opportunity to preach to them of Jesus and the great salvation. A brief prayer was then offered and Venkappah, the first Telugu convert, was led down into the water and baptized into the name of the Father, Son, and Holy Ghost. It was a strange sight to the wondering multitude, but a happy experience to Venkappah, and probably one of the most blessed privileges of Mr. Day's life." This was the first of many thousands who were to follow, but before the brightness of the day could come, a miniature dark age must intervene. Soon his only associate missionary broke down in health and had to leave the country. The cholera broke out and began sweeping the people into eternity. Soon his own health failed and he, too, was compelled to leave for his native land. He left with a very sad heart. What would become of the work he had begun, only begun? O, the dark hours! He wrote on leaving: "The thought of visiting one's own native country gives little satisfaction." As he left those dark shores and needy people, his heart lingered with them. But, ere long, he was permitted to return, and with him came to the Telugus, Dr. Lyman Jewett, one of the most devoted men of God who ever carried the Gospel across the seas. He and his faithful wife went earnestly into the work, soon acquired the language and traveled among the villages. But few converts were gathered, however, as the months and years went by. Great faith in God was eminently needed; for then in all their labors they must indeed walk by faith and not by sight. Thirteen years had passed since the mission was established, and only a little handful of converts were to show for all their labor and expenditure.

CHAPTER X.

The Break of Day: Triumph of the Gospel.

At a meeting of the Board held in Albany, New York, in 1853, it was proposed to abandon the Telugu mission altogether. A warm discussion followed, during which one of the speakers pointed to a missionary map which hung on the wall behind him and said: "Behold the lone star!" In all that dark land there was but one spot from which a single ray of Gospel light could eminate. Dr. Smith was so impressed with the words "lone star" that ere he slept that night he wrote the following beautiful and truly prophetic lines:

> Shine on, "Lone Star," thy radiance bright
> Shall spread o'er all the eastern sky;
> Morn breaks apace from gloom and night;
> Shine on and bless the pilgrim's eye.
>
> Shine on, "Lone Star," I would not dim
> The light that burns with dubious ray;
> The lonely star of Bethlehem,
> Led on a bright and glorious day.

Shine on, "Lone Star," in grief and tears,
And sad reverses oft baptized.
Shine on amid thy sister spheres;
Lone stars in heaven are not despised.

Shine on, "Lone Star," the day draws near,
When none shall shine more fair than thou;
Thou, born and nursed in doubt and fear,
Wilt glitter on Immanuel's brow.

Shine on, "Lone Star," till earth redeemed,
In dust shall bid its idols fall;
And thousands where thy radiance beamed
Shall "crown the Savior, Lord of all."

This poem was read next morning at the Board meeting. The effect was extraordinary; hearts were moved and tears flowed freely. The discussion was discontinued and it was decided, not only to continue the mission to the Telegus, but to reinforce it. Almost the same day those discussions were going on in Albany, New York, the work in India took on new life. The little church in Nellore was reorganized, and a number more were baptized. Now, this was the gray of the dawn. Better times must follow. Dr. and Mrs. Jewett toured extensively among the distant villages and preached the Word. Other missionaries were sent out from home, and now the mission to the Telugus was no longer a doubtful experience. But the field was so large for the laborers, they were greatly burdened and ceased not to pray to God and petition the people at home for stronger reinforcements. They were sent out as fast as the committee could command the men and means. The people heard the Gospel a little more willingly, and the fruit began to ripen. The Nellore church grew to considerable strength; but the work must be extended into other districts, and as Dr. and Mrs. Jewett make a tour into the North, let us spend a little time with them in Ongole. It was about four o'clock New Year's morning, 1854, that Dr. and Mrs. Jewett, with a little company of native Christians might have been seen passing out of their tents and wending their way toward the mountain overlooking Ongole. At the base of this hill on the eastern side, lies the crescent shaped town of Ongole, with its ten thousand people. Standing on the summit of this hill in the morning light the scene is truly sublime. The country is a broad, level plain, spread out before the eye, like a wondrous panorama. Turning around, the eye may behold no less than four hundred villages, which, with their groves of margosa trees, dot the broad expanse in every direction. Ten miles to the east lies the bay of Bengal, forming a blue border along the horizon. Sixty miles to the west, rise up the dim heads of a mountain range; thirty miles to the south stretches out the silverlike belt of the Buckingham canal; while forty miles away under the Northern sky, the blue mountains tower like pillars of cloud. Within this compass live no less than a million of souls, bound for eternity. The sight is enough to impress the non-emotional. In the early light this little company, Dr. and Mrs. Jewett and the native Christians, Julia, Ruth and Christian Nursu, the only Gospel witnesses in all that land, ascended the mountain. Reaching the summit they sat down and sang a hymn. Then they all knelt while Nursu prayed for his lost countrymen. Dr. Jewett then read from Isaiah: "How beautiful upon the mountains are the feet of him that bringeth good tidings." Mrs. Jewett then prayed, then Julia, then Ruth.

Last of all the faithful leader of this little band lifted up his voice and said: "O, thou Creator and God of the nations, grant that as the sun is now about to rise, and shine upon the earth, so may the sun of Righteousness rise quickly and shine upon this dark land." He prayed also for God to send a missionary to preach the Gospel to the perishing millions around him. Then, rising, he stretched forth his hand and said, "Do you see that piece of rising ground yonder all covered over with prickly pears? Would you not like that spot for our mission bungalow, and all this land to become Christian? How would you like it? Well, Nursu, Julia, that day will come!" "As our little prayer meeting closed," Julia said, "the sun rose, and it seemed as if the Holy Spirit had lifted us above the world, and our hearts were filled with thanksgiving to the Lord."

We have only to look over that field to-day to see the answer to that prayer, and the fulfillment of that prediction. The mission bungalow stands on the very spot that he pointed out and, though the land has not yet become Christian, it is going on towards it. There is now in Ongole the largest church in the world, it having over twenty thousand members. The work which has brought about such great results has been led on chiefly by Dr. J. E. Clough. He was the one sent out in answer to Dr. Jewett's prayer, though the answer seemed long delayed. He came to Ongole the 17th of September, 1866, and at once began the work which has done so much for the glory of Christ's name and the salvation of the heathen. We shall not find it consistent with the plan of this little book to follow in detail the wonderful works of God among the Telugus.* We only stand in awe and glance over the field and the great hosts of God there, like a proud soldier beholding the splendid regiments of his chieftain. The native workers rapidly increased in number. Who ever accepted Christ went to work in his own village to lead his people to the Savior.. So the Gospel went, as it were, on wings; men heard and

---

*If anyone desires a full and detailed account of the work and workers among the Telugus, he is referred to Mr. Downie's History of the Telugu Mission, published by the American Baptist Publication Society.

believed. New stations were established as rapidly as possible, but at length the interest seemed to center in Ongole and the power of the Gospel seemed to radiate from that center, not, as we believe, so much because Dr. Clough was in himself such an extraordinary man, though he is a man of no common ability, and was raised up for that field and work. Dr. Downie says of him, very properly we think: "If we were called upon to mention Dr. Clough's special qualification to the particular work to which he has been called, we should say they were these: a capacity to command the situation and to marshal its resources; a sound constitution and an indomitable spirit; a strong love for the souls of men and for Christ; a successful term of service in the Western States, and a strong faith both in God and in himself as God's appointed agent for the accomplishment of a great work." Answered in the life and work of Dr. Clough, we believe the prayers of the devoted Dr. Jewett were at the head of the great movement among the Telegus. After his return to America it was said of him that for a great many nights his wife was unintentionally waked as he rose from bed near midnight and went into another room alone. At last she passed into the hall and watched him. She saw him walking the floor, his silvered beard on his breast and his arms folded, exclaiming in pathetic and trembling voice: "Oh God, do save the Telugus!" Such prayers will be heard.

In 1876 the great famine broke out in India and sore distress prevailed. Thousands starved to death. Disease smote the already famished land, and the people fell by thousands into dreadful graves. But, in it all, the people were convinced of the utter inability of their idols to afford them relief, and so were more disposed to listen to the Gospel. It was preached everywhere over the Ongole field, and during the famine, though many applied, none were received into the church for fear some might come from unworthy motives. But when the blessing of God began to restore plenty once more in the land, the doors of the church were opened. Dr. Clough sent out word to all his native preachers to bring in those who desired to be baptized, and they would meet ten miles north of Ongole on the Gundalacumma river. When they began to pour in from all sides the magnitude of the ingathering was beginning to be manifest. The candidates were all examined, and when everything was ready they appointed six o'clock next morning to begin baptizing. It was the third of July and the sun rose in all his brilliancy; the people thronged the banks of the river, and two ordained native preachers took their places in the water. They began baptizing, and the people passed in a constant stream into the river by them, were baptized, and came up out of the water. When these two preachers were tired, two others took their places, and in turn were succeeded by others. At eleven o'clock they stopped for the noon rest; resumed their work at two, and at five o'clock the last of two thousand two hundred and twenty-two was buried with Christ in baptism. Thus by only six men, two working at a time, the whole number were baptized in eight hours. Thus closed a day of sublime victory for Christ. But the battle ceased not, and the victory grew on in magnitude. More and more kept coming in until, before the last of the following December, they had baptized nine thousand six hundred and six.

During the years that have followed, that great revival has never ceased; though, of course, not as brilliant as the above. The reports of this ingathering roused our people at home as never before. The glad news fairly shook this Christian land, and God's people were encouraged in their contributions to such a noble work and their prayers were daily offered. The next largest number baptized was that in which the writer had the privilege of assisting. It was shortly after our arrival in India, in 1890. A deep spiritual interest was everywhere manifest among the native workers and they seemed full of enthusiasm and hope. They gave glowing reports from all the out-stations how the people heard the Gospel gladly, and great numbers were believing. Dr. Clough told them to bring in to the quarterly meeting all those who were asking baptism. Saturday evening, the 23d of December, they began to pour into the mission compound. Many came on foot across the burning sands from fifty to seventy miles away. Early Sunday morning Dr. Clough rang the school bell and called the people all together around his veranda in the yard. Nearly four thousand people were seated on the ground under the beautiful margosa shade trees. Dr. Clough, in whom they all reposed so much confidence, then stood on the veranda and preached to them from the text: "Come unto me all ye that labor and are heavy laden, and I will give you rest." It was so appropriate; and the people listened for an hour and ten minutes with the deepest interest. Then followed the examination of the candidates, lasting till a late hour. The examination was conducted by committees, including altogether about a hundred native preachers. One o'clock was appointed to begin baptizing, and at that hour an immense throng of Telugus, both heathen and Christian, gathered around the beautiful pool just east of the mission house. The tall margosa drooped its limbs down over the water, and around the garden occasional cocoanut trees lifted up their straight proud forms. It was a sublime hour. Two ordained preachers took their places in the pool, and after a song they proceeded in the glorious work. They baptized over a thousand; then Dr. Clough and the writer took their places and baptized over six-hundred, making in all, sixteen hundred and seventy-one; and the exact time occupied in immersing the entire number was just four hours and twenty-five minutes.

Thus closed another day long to be remembered in the history of missions; a day wherein the Lord Christ was honored and the heathen stood silent and amazed in the presence of the mighty works of God.

It has often been asked me since our return to this country; "How do those people hold out?" My answer has always been, "As well as the people do in this country." And that is saying a great deal for the Telugus; for if they, with all their weakness, bad habits formed from their youth, lack of knowledge, no restraining society, but powerful temptations all around them, if they can hold out as well as converts in this country, where they have had Christian training and have the protection of Christian society, do they not deserve greater credit than Americans? And is not their salvation a greater miracle of divine grace? All praise to the saving power that can reach down to the low and degraded and lift them up. Is it not a stronger proof of the divinity of the Christian religion to see it go down to a man all degraded to the depths of shame in the darkest ignorance and save his soul, lift him up to a righteous life, a good degree of intelligence and happiness, than to see that same religion save an intelligent, refined gentleman or lady in our own society? Yea, it speaks volumes for that religion which is adapted to the conditions and needs of all mankind. Christ's religion does save the Hindu, and the Chinese, and the African, and the American, all alike, and it saves them for time and eternity. It changes the very appearance of the Telugu. He is cleaner, more cheerful, more bright, and his life among the heathen is a living example and proof of the power of Christ to save. The heathen often give names to our Christians, such as *"prarthana chasa vwadu"*—the praying man. In Hanamakonda, one of our men who is now an efficient preacher, was once a thief, robber and adulterer. He was known throughout the country for his wickedness.

But some years ago he was converted. Now, when a missionary goes into his or any surrounding village and tells of the power of Christ to save, the heathen will readily answer: "Yes, we know your religion does change a man; for we all knew Sundriah. He was a very wicked man, but since he has become a Christian we have never seen him do anything bad. He used to whip and abuse his family, but now he loves them and talks kindly to his wife."

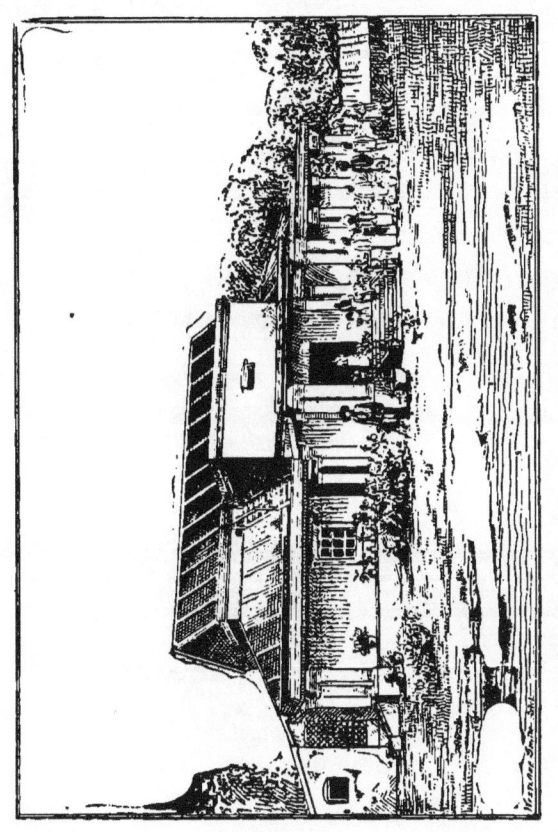

MISSION BUNGALOW, HANAMAKONDA, INDIA.

CHAPTER XI.

Shadows Begin to Deepen: Sickness and Death.

In November, 1891, we took charge of the Hanamakonda mission field. The church was small and the workers were very few. In fact, there were only three unordained native preachers. The station had been nearly two years without a resident missionary, and the work of the station was still a pioneer work. Though with only a limited command of the language we began. The work in and immediately around the station demanded our chief attention, so that but little touring among the native villages could be done that season. The study of the language was continued. The hot weather came on in February, and in March our baby Ola, being teething, was taken quite severely with bronchitis. We tried every means within our power to relieve him, but in vain. We then took him to Secunderabad city, eighty miles from our station, where we obtained the medical services of an English army surgeon.

For one whole month we remained in the city, and the doctor attended faithfully to his charge, but our precious love grew no better, but rather worse. The heat was terrible, and the doctor at last said he could do no more for him and gave him up, saying the only hope of saving his life was to take him immediately to a cooler climate. Our hearts were sad; but still hoping we started at once for Bangalore city, a summer resort which lies far up on the western Ghauts, or mountain range. Obtaining the services of a good physician, we kept the little sufferer there over two months. He seemed to improve. Hope revived; still his double teeth were giving him trouble. Finally the extreme heat broke on the plains. The June and July rains had come, and the air was much cooler. The work at the station was urgently demanding our presence and attention. The physician said we might, without increasing the danger, take our babe back to the station. I came on a few days ahead, leaving the faithful nurse to assist Mrs. Johnson to make the journey, and spent the time in cleansing and whitewashing our house.

A sad experience awaited my return to the mission compound. The oldest child of one of my best native preachers was taken very ill with fever, which was at that time so prevalent among the natives. For two days and nights we waited on the dear little boy doing all that was possible to save him. But it was not the will of the Father. Late in the evening of July the 6th, while his father was gone to the hospital for medicine, the little spirit went home to heaven. The mother was on her knees in the yard crying very bitterly when her husband entered the gate. He knew what was the matter for he had been expecting it. The great tears rolled down his cheeks as he approached her. He took her by the hand and lifted her up and said in the sweetest Christian spirit, "Let us not weep, it is God's will." Next morning the little body was quietly laid in the grave. As we all stood around, the Bible had been read, a hymn had been sung, and we were about ready to lower the body into its last resting place, an incident occurred which gave me a more exalted idea of the Telugu Christian character than anything I had witnessed before or have ever seen since. A great company of heathen were standing around the little cemetery and a number of sympathizing Christian friends stood around the grave. Henry, the father of the departed, asked to speak. I told him to speak on. He then stepped forward with uplifted hands, weeping, and prayed to God most earnestly for divine comfort and strength. When he had prayed he began to speak, and proceeded in one of the most eloquent short addresses I ever heard fall from human lips. It was in words that I was most familiar with and I understood it all. It so well illustrates the native eloquence of that beautiful language and the sublime conception of the simple Christian heart, that I attempted a literal translation of the address. The following, though I am certain does not do it justice, is as near what he said as one could get from memory:

"My brothers and sisters in our Lord Jesus Christ, weeping, we have come here this morning to lay into the grave all that can ever perish of the child of my love. We are ready to put into the grave this dear little body and say good-bye to it for a little while, But we know we shall meet again. O, that all my benighted countrymen only had this hope and joy. Great God of all the world, help us to preach this blessed word to the people. O, how glorious, our sweet Savior, that we have learned to know thee. Thou hast taken our child away from the sins and sorrows of this dark world. We would catch hold of thy golden feet and fall down forever before thee. He was mine, but God gave him, and now he has taken him from us. As I see that face now before me, cold and still, I do not see the face of my son. That is not my son now. My child has left that form and has been for several hours up there. O, glorious world! My child and my Savior are there this morning, and their silver wings sparkle in the shining light; O, I would that I could go now and be with them, but I must wait a little." Then coming nearer his child he kissed the cold features and said: "Good-bye now, for a while; but when Jesus calls, we will all go, and in that golden city, where death never comes, I will take you back to my arms, and Jesus shall wipe away our tears."

That such joy and hope might be implanted in one Hindu breast, is itself worth all the money and labor it has ever cost to send the Gospel to the heathen.

The death of this dear little one was a trial to all of us, but by it we were brought nearer the Lord and were incited to do more for him.

Mrs. Johnson arrived with our little boy the very night the other lay a corpse in the compound. Though apparently better, he was much exhausted by the long journey. We began at once to make preparations for touring, as the season was almost at hand. Some camp tables, chairs and cots were to be made. I had a few tools; so got the wood, hired a native carpenter to assist me, and we went to work. I found it all but impossible to get any native even to hold, in a different way from what he was accustomed to do, a piece of wood while I sawed it. They have but one way of doing anything, and they never imagine it could be done any other way. They all do as they were taught by their parents before them. So I had to do the most of the work myself. Rungiah, one of my best preachers, was a great help to me. We were rapidly getting things together and planning for extensive Gospel touring. But the divine plan had marked our way along paths more rugged than we had ever traveled. Just one week after the night our watch was kept over the native brother's child, we were called upon to wade the river of sorrow through the silent darkness. Our day's work was done. Mrs. Johnson and I were sitting in the room talking about our precious little one. He had been quite cheerful all that day, and enjoyed playing with a little monkey we had bought for him. We talked of his long struggle, his near approach to death, and of his recovery. We talked of his future and what we might be able to do for him. We then bowed in our evening prayer. While we were in prayer the baby began crying, as his nurse was preparing his food in an adjoining room. When the prayer was finished his mother took him in her arms, and in three minutes his voice was hushed and the immortal spirit of our loved one was gone. He had died thus suddenly from heart failure. In the heat his body could not endure the ordeal of teething, and his strength gave way. What should we do? Secunderabad was eighty miles away and to bury our treasure in our own station, no hand but the natives could assist us in the last hour, and a plain box must answer for a coffin. So we determined to go into the city. We were four miles from the railroad. In our tears we prepared for the trip. He died at half-past eight and the train passed the station at half-past eleven. I then took all that was mortal of our beloved, and in my arms carried him to the station, and all night long we watched by him as he lay on the seat in the car, until we arrived in the city next morning. The darkness of that night, in a lonely heathen land with none to comfort or sympathize, save the God who had afflicted us, none may ever know, save those who have passed through the same firey trial. May all our friends be ever saved from such a trial. With the help of friends we laid the little body to rest in the cemetery just west of that great city, Hyderabad. There, almost beneath the shadows of three score Mohammedan mosques, the body of our dear little Ola awaits the coming of the Savior and a glorious resurrection.

Mrs. Johnson was soon taken with fever, and our touring was still delayed. During all this time the work around Hanamakonda was carried on as vigorously as possible, and several were believing. Fifteen were baptized before we started on tour. By and by, all was ready and, with our native helpers, we started out on our Gospel tour. Our first trip was to a town thirty miles from our station. Here we remained only a short while and preached the Gospel; but success attended our efforts and we baptized five of the leading men, who boldly came out on the Lord's side.

We then returned home and prepared for a more extensive work. Moncota, a very important part of our field, eighty miles away to the southeast, was hitherto unworked, and we resolved to go there. Tent, table, cot and camp chairs and all our dishes and cooking vessels gathered up, put in carts, our house and compound left in charge of one of the preachers who remained to care for the church in the station, we were off on our way.

to parts where, by many, the Gospel had never been heard. We arrived in Moncota on the seventh of September, and pitched our tent in a large mango grove. It was in the midst of the tiger reservation where the Nizam had for years been accustomed to pitch his tent on occasions of his annual "*chicari*," or hunt. From our tent we went out for several days and preached first in the town nearest by us. Then we began to go out to neighboring villages all around us, and so preached the word of God through all the country round about. Everywhere the people listened with respect and in some places with great curiosity. Sometimes fear would keep many away. In Moncota, our message was received with great earnestness, and after several days of preaching and prayer with them, seven of the leading men of the Madaga caste professed faith in Christ. The next morning they were received and baptized.

One of them was a spotted leper. By covering our hands with carbolic soap, we baptized him without fear of contagion. The country is full of leprosy, and there seems to be no law to prohibit lepers from mixing in society with other people. Everyone takes his chances, but many believe that not half of the leprosy is contagious. In fact, leprous parents have been known to raise perfectly healthy children. There is one kind which is certainly contagious, however, that where the flesh is decayed, and we have often seen them with their fingers and toes entirely gone; poor helpless beggars. It seemed that at the time those seven men were baptized almost the whole village would become Christians. The interest seemed so deep. But the devil was at work. The morning of the baptizing we induced the converts to have their long hair cut off. It was dirty, as usual, and their appearance would be greatly improved by its removal. Besides, the Hindus often wear a long tuft of hair called "juttu," on the back of their heads. It is believed by many to be a sign of heathen worship. This, as is required by the missionaries, must be removed on becoming Christians. The men willingly consented to have their hair trimmed nicely; but when they returned to their village the Mohammedans started the alarm that the missionary had come as a secret agent to capture all the people, men and women, cut off their hair and ship it away as an article of merchandise. This report created a general panic among the women especially; for they prize their hair very highly. It would be an awful disgrace for a Hindu woman to have her hair cut closely. The next morning early when we entered the village, not a dozen would come to meet us. We could see men, women and children, when we approached, skipping around the house corners and peeping back after us. As we came nearer they continued to retreat to other houses more remote and watched us from the corners. But soon those we had baptized came out with sorrowful faces, and told us the story of their trouble. We could then do but little more with the heathen there. The Mohammedans continued their falsehoods and threats until the poor people were afraid to see us. We induced them before we left, however, to send one of their leading men to our headquarters and find out all about us from the people where we lived. He returned with a favorable report which gave the lie to all the Mohammedans had told them, and henceforth the people were a little more friendly disposed; but could not, while we remained, get entirely over their fright.

We very much enjoyed camp life at first; but finally the jackals began every night to set up their yelling immediately around our tent, and our sleep was continually broken. Then came the monkeys by the hundred. They literally filled the trees all around us and chattered until often we could not have heard thunder. Then the rain began to pour down upon us. The time for the rains to cease had long since passed; unexpectedly, however, they came. For four days and nights, almost incessantly, the rain poured down upon us. At last, when we were all in danger of dying in the damp tent, we pulled up in the rain and left for a station forty miles up the railroad, where we could get on higher ground and find a house to shelter us. We had no more than reached this station when one after another of our native preachers began falling sick with the malarial fever and chills. For some days we did nothing but doctor the sick. In the meantime the rain had ceased, and we began to hope. We removed to a station still nearer home. We sent one of our best preachers, A. Rungiah, to Secunderabad city for some supplies. While there he fell sick with a severe fever and could not get home. At one time all our native preachers and servants were down except one, and he was hardly able to walk about. Last of all, Mrs. Johnson took the fever, and I alone, through the mercy of God, was left to wait on the sick. But I could not risk myself to doctor her, besides I myself might take the same fever at anytime. So we got on the train and went into the city where the services of a physician could be had. Mrs. Johnson was then almost past standing alone. We went to a boarding house, and at once sent for an English physician. After caring for Mrs. Johnson, my next duty was to hunt up my poor native preacher, who was lying near death's door. I found him praying. He said he had given up to die, if it were God's will, but he said he almost knew I would come to his relief that day; for he had prayed constantly for four days and nights for God to send me to him, and if I did not come that

ATHMAKUR RUNGIAH.

day, he felt that he must die, for he was only growing worse. He did not know, however, that I was within eighty miles of him, or that I had any intention of coming to the city. When I entered the little veranda, on which he was lying, and spoke to him, without turning his head, though so weak, he lifted his hands toward heaven and said: "O, God, I bless thee that thou hast answered my prayer." Then he looked me in the face, as he took my hand, and such expressions of gratitude I never saw, as then lit up his poor face. He said he knew then that he was saved. I hurried off immediately for a good doctor. No one had ever called a doctor or given him scarcely a bite to eat. The doctor came, gave him some good medicines, and left directions about his food. I then hired some natives to wait on him, give his medicine, and prepare and give him the proper kind of food. In a few days I was greatly surprised to see him able to walk, and he was among the happiest men on earth. The native treatment of diseases deserves special mention; not, however, that the medical fraternity of America might gain thereby much valuable information, but more fully to show another heathen extreme. India boasts very loudly of her former knowledge and claims especially to have led the world in the medical science. She says: "The Occident sat at her feet and learned of her the knowledge of medicine." But if she ever had cause to boast, she now has abundant reason to cover her face in shame. There are many native so-called doctors, and their medicines and methods of treatment are as different as the doctors themselves. Many of them make fluids of certain herbs and may occasionally give that which is needed to cure the disease. But they have no knowledge of physiology or hygiene, and usually are so extreme that they permanently injure or kill more than they cure. For example, they often pour the strongest kinds of fluids in the eyes and ears, in place of the mouth, to cure the colic or other stomach troubles. It seems almost too ridiculous to tell; but for its truth we have the word of our medical missionaries who have had extensive practice among the people. They often tie the poor sick down on one side, from which position they must not move for long periods. Various other ridiculous performances are ordered. For what reason, I know not, unless to appear to know something and to be officious. Sometimes they give nothing but sand, and the ignorant people in their distress take it in perfect faith. There was one instance that was quite familiar to our Madras missionaries, where a woman was actually ordered to, and did, drink three quarts of cow dung, in order to be relieved of a devil that was supposed to possess her ! !

When we were on tour, and one of our native helpers had taken the chills and fever, I went out at night to give some medicine before retiring. I saw this man sitting in the midst of the tent in perfect agony, while another was down in front thrusting a pin up under his great toe nail and filling the hole thus made with a virulent poison extracted from some weed. The poor man had been taught, in his heathen state, to believe that a course of such treatment would cure the chills and fever. Medical missionaries are greatly needed in India, and they are among the most successful of our workers in leading the people to Christ.

CHAPTER XII.
The Sad Farewell: Homeward Voyage: Storm at Sea.

Poor Mrs. Johnson was still suffering. For two weeks she struggled with that dreadful jungle fever before it began to give way. She was not able to gain strength. She remained in the city under the care of the doctor till the last of November. The doctor had repeatedly told us that her recovery in India was doubtful. The annual conference or association of the Deccan missionaries and native churches met in Palmoor, the first of December. By that time Mrs. Johnson had gained sufficient strength to go to the conference; as we thought a trip across the country in the open air would help her. The weather was cool enough then to be pleasant. After we arrived in Palmoor she seemed to grow no better. Mr. Maplesden then came sorrowfully to me and said that the doctor in Secunderabad had told him immediately before leaving the city that his final conclusion was that Mrs. Johnson's recovery in India was impossible, and begged him to urge us to leave the country at once. The whole conference of missionaries said we had better go without delay. Then came a burden that was equalled by only one other in life. We must say good bye to our work—which had been only fairly begun. We must say farewell to our loved native people, which in truth was a far greater trial than leaving our friends in the homeland. Our friends at home could well get along without us; but in India they needed us and we were bound to them, and to our work, by the strongest ties. How could we break them? How could we leave the land which had entombed our loved one? But the Lord had called on us to do so. Just as the sun went down, we all gathered in the yard under a mango tree. I then announced to my dear preachers the unanimous decision of the conference, and of us all, that we must leave at once for America. Sad tears and mutual expressions of love from us all showed ties that were hard to be broken. But we must submit to our father's will; though we can't always see why he demands of us so much. Though we can't understand his ways, we must leave it all to Him and, trusting, obey his voice.

With aching hearts we took our farewell and turned our faces toward Bombay. But Rungiah, who was so sick in the city, would not leave us. In his devotion he wanted, even, to follow us to America and declared he would live and die with me. I must confess that I have never met but few men on earth that I loved so well. He is such a devoted, sincere Christian, so humble, so Christ-like, that to know him is to love him. He is also an able man; he can read, write and speak fluently, four different languages: Telugu, Tamil, Hindustani and English. He was permitted to go with us to Bombay and stay to see us on the steamer. We then pointed him to his lost countrymen, whom he was so useful in leading to Christ, and as we bade him good-bye, assured him of our prayers and constant love. His picture shows the manly features of one of the noblest of the Telugus.

Henry, also, who lost his little boy the summer before, was Rungiah's equal in most respects, and we shall always thank God for those two devoted servants of the Lord.

December the 17th, 1892, on board the steamer "Ganges" of the Peninsular and Oriental line, we looked for the last time upon the coral strands of that spiritually dark land, and the Arabian Sea lay out before us. To cheer our hearts in the sad hour, we tried to turn our thoughts to the homeland and loved ones far beneath the setting sun. We started out writing poetry, but returning now, it had all fled from us. In our cheerlessness we said:

"O, that a song would sing itself to me!"
We felt so sad and disappointed.

In our homeward voyage, we encountered a fearful storm. For two days and nights the fury of the winds hung over us, and threatened destruction. It was in the Mediterranean Sea, shortly after leaving the island of Malta we came into the gale which swept down upon us in dreadful power. The sea rolled high, the waves leaped into the sky, broke and fell in the beating winds like sheets of driven rain. Our ship rolled and plunged like a mad beast. We would go to the crest of a great wave like mounting high on a hill top, then as the wave fell another great one was gathering ahead, and when we plunged to the great trough below, a mighty wave rolled over us which for a while altogether buried us under the angry sea. When we came up the heavens were dark with fury above us and the seething ocean prepared again to swallow us into its awful depths. There was no cursing on board that ship, no idle song was heard, no vain word uttered. Children crying, women weeping as they sent up their repeated prayers to the God of the ocean, and strong men who never bowed the knee before were calling on the Almighty God for mercy.

Yes, men will pray. People, in their fruitless attempts to move about, run their heads against posts and walls; the dishes fly from the table and break in heaps in some corner of the room. So the dreadful tumult goes on.

When, on the third morning the sun rose clear and beautiful, the sea calm, and we were all saved, devout hearts gave thanks to God,
"Who plants his footsteps in the sea
And rides upon the storm."

The trip to England was made at last, and we were snugly quartered in the Shaftsbury Hotel for a few days rest. The cold in England was most severe on us. I had, after going on the ship, given up to the malaria, which had for so many weeks been trying in vain to make me its victim. The Lord had certainly given me strength to withstand it in order that I might care for others; but now that we were under different circumstances, there was no reason why I should not suffer as others had. I was sick during nearly all the voyage to England and that, added to the storm, made the voyage anything but a pleasant one.

As we sped over the Atlantic at last our thoughts began to turn more engagingly toward the home land; toward the old home and loved ones. In our travels in other lands we had learned to love our own country, for there is none like her in all the borders of the earth. Dawned our last morning at sea. We were two hundred miles off New York. The ship seemed to plough the Atlantic all too slowly. But finally, 'twas past noon, we gazed steadily toward the west and saw, in the distance, the outlines of our homeland. We thanked God. There came to us as never before, those words:

> My native country, thee,
> Land of the noble free,
> Thy name I love;
> I love thy rocks and rills,
> Thy woods and templed hills;
> My heart with rapture thrills,
> Like that above.

Then,

"Like the benediction that follows after prayer,"

fell upon our hearts the sweet strains of

"Home, sweet home!"

And we were soon there.

www.ingramcontent.com/pod-product-compliance
Lightning Source LLC
Chambersburg PA
CBHW031456160426
43195CB00010BB/999